The World of
POLDARK

The World of
POLDARK

Emma Marriott

A Mammoth Screen production for BBC and MASTERPIECE™

St. Martin's Press
New York

THE *POLDARK* NOVELS

Also by Winston Graham:

The Rev. Stebbing Shaw, *A Tour to the West of England* (1788)

All the ranks in this county are very sociable, generous and kind to each other; being bounded on all sides, except Devon, by the sea, emigrations and intermixtures with other counties are less frequent than in other parts of the kingdom; so that they usually marry amongst themselves, whence comes the proverb 'that all Cornish gentlemen are cousins'. It is the same in Wales; where the greatest compliment amongst one another in the same country is the appellation of cousin. There is a great conformity of manners, customs &c between the Welch and Cornish, as well as similarity in their ancient languages, but the latter is more lost. I was greatly pleased to see the respect and veneration which the lower class in this town have for the gentlemen around them from whose assistance and protection they seem to derive a greater share of happiness than I ever heard expressed in any other place.

CONTENTS

FOREWORD

by screenwriter and executive producer
DEBBIE HORSFIELD

I first became involved with *Poldark* when the Mammoth Screen producers Karen Thrussell and Damien Timmer approached me to ask whether I might consider adapting the first two *Poldark* novels, *Ross Poldark* and *Demelza*. Having never done an adaptation before – almost everything else I've written has been contemporary – my initial reaction was to think they had asked the wrong person! Nevertheless I took the books away on holiday – and had read all of three pages before I was hooked. I came home and said yes without hesitation.

Once on board, my first task was to read all twelve of Winston Graham's *Poldark* books in order to get an idea of the journeys of the characters and the overall story arcs. The next task was to decide how many books to go for on the first series. Originally the BBC commissioned six episodes but I soon realized that this wouldn't be enough to do justice to the complexities of narrative and character so we went back and asked for eight episodes and thankfully the BBC agreed.

During the first few months of script development I did a lot of background reading: the history of the period, both British and world history, books about the mining and fishing industries in Cornwall, about the Methodist movement, about the conditions that gave rise to smuggling, etc. I listened to the

music of the period, both classical and folk. It also helped that my degree is in English Literature so I was very familiar with the literature of the period, also with the vocabulary, idioms, phrases, manners, etiquette, traditions, etc.

In addition, I talked a lot with our brilliant historical advisor Dr Hannah Greig, Lecturer in History at York University, specializing in eighteenth-century studies. She looked at the scripts to check the historical content, flagging any areas that might need some adjustment or adding in a bit of historical detail here and there. Hannah also went to rehearsals to meet the cast and talk about eighteenth-century history, the context of the period, human experiences, mannerisms and culture and any questions that came up from the cast.

Andrew Graham, the author's son, has been unfailingly supportive – and very hands on. Every key decision is run by him and we have been in constant contact from the script stage onwards. He reads all the scripts and gives feedback. We also consult with him on major casting and creative decisions.

One of my main concerns from the outset was to do justice to the novels. Winston Graham is a masterly storyteller and his characters are wonderful creations. In a way I felt the same weight of expectation as I might have done if I had adapted a Jane Austen or a Dickens novel – not because of the many other adaptations that might be compared to it but because of wanting to do justice to the original material. I hadn't watched the 1970s series, and opted not to do so until I'd written most of the scripts. In any case I and the team at Mammoth Screen were clear that we were creating something new rather than remaking a previous version, so whilst it was interesting to see the 1970s incarnation – and totally get why it was so popular! – it didn't feature in any of our decision-making. Obviously though, we were aware of its huge popularity, and hoped that fans would find something to enjoy in the new adaptation. And what's been exciting is that there's a whole generation which had never seen – or in some cases even heard of – the first series, so for them we started with a clean slate.

Above right: *Director Ed Bazalgette and Debbie Horsfield.*
Below right: *Filming in Corsham, Wiltshire.*

The narratives of the *Poldark* novels are multi-stranded with characters which are so beautifully drawn you feel they could actually walk into the room. The stories themselves are both epic in their sweep and exquisitely detailed in the creation of their world. They are set against a backdrop of great historical, social, economic turbulence – and they deal with compelling themes such as ambition, rivalry, betrayal, family and of course, love. When I first read them I was reminded of Margaret Mitchell's *Gone With the Wind*, which is similarly a portrait of a society at a time of great change, with an epic love story at its heart and a cast of unforgettable characters.

A key element of *Poldark*, of course, is Ross Poldark. He is one of literature's great heroes: a gentleman who is also a rebel, who has a keen sense of morality and social justice but without any priggishness or moralizing. He's also a great romantic figure – caught between two women from two completely different backgrounds. A gentleman who marries his kitchen maid. A man who doesn't stand on ceremony, who doesn't play by the rules and often falls foul of authority. He has elements of Darcy, Heathcliff, Rochester, Rhett Butler and Robin Hood – quite a combination!

Cornwall also is central to *Poldark*. I'd had several holidays in Cornwall and had always loved the wild elemental nature of its landscape and the extreme weather – the landscape and weather play a huge part in the novels and we've done our best to capture those extremes. The summer we filmed (2014) was one of the

sunniest for many years and Cornwall looks gorgeous (although the very first scenes we shot in Cornwall were in March 2014 during the storms so we got some spectacular footage of waves). On the other hand, sometimes the weather was *too* sunny! On one memorable occasion the script called for 'angry waves' and what we got instead was a flat, calm, turquoise-blue sea which looked like the Aegean!

My aim has always been to make sure that what the readers love so much about the books – the vividness of the characterization, the complexity of the storytelling – is translated to the screen. This obviously means getting the casting and the creation of the *Poldark* 'world' right. We think we've assembled an amazing cast who do justice to Winston Graham's characters. And we also hope the world we've created, from Catrin Mereddyd's production design to Marianne Agertoft's costumes and Jacqueline Fowler's hair and make-up, also has authenticity as well as beauty and style. Series one has been an extraordinary adventure for all of us and we're looking forward to continuing our journey through Winston Graham's incredible saga.

Debbie Horsfield

ELIZABETH

*'Pray do not
be reckless, I wish
you to return.'*

ROSS

'It won't be for long.'

ELIZABETH

'You'll forget me.'

ROSS

'Never!'

CHAPTER ONE

The year is 1783 and Ross Poldark returns from the American War of Independence to his beloved Cornwall. Drained from funding costly wars overseas, Britain is in the grip of a recession, with rising prices and high taxes, falling wages, and a bubbling of social unrest. Cornwall is hit particularly hard, and only the bankers seem to be making money as once-booming mines close and debts rise. Amid this turmoil, Ross comes back to a home in ruins: his father dead and his childhood sweetheart engaged to his cousin and best friend – his own heart as battered as the country around him.

The world of the Poldarks is not an easy one to inhabit. Life expectancy in the eighteenth century is just thirty-seven years – even less in many Cornish mining communities – and a third of children never see their fifth birthday. It's a brutal world: petty criminals are publicly flogged, hanged or left to rot in prison; blood sports remain a popular pastime amongst every class; and animals and the poor are worked into the ground. The cogs of the industrial revolution, oiled by the growth in banking, are on the turn, and there is money to be made, lots of it. A few do well, rising up the social ladder, but the bulk of the population remain in poverty, many simply scratching a living on the edge of starvation. Social hierarchy, bolstered by an intricate system of custom, deference, and local and family loyalties, is the natural order of the day – and the gulf between the haves and have-nots, the propertied and unpropertied, is still vast.

Out of this complex and difficult world emerges Ross Poldark, a character who seems to exemplify the resilience of the human spirit, a man able to fight back at all that is thrown at him. Limping and bearing a scar to his face, Ross returns from three years of fighting in a war, during which we learn of his reckless past, escaping the gallows despite 'brawling, free trading and assaulting a customs official'. Though born a gentleman, there is a rebellious side to Ross's nature – but at heart he has integrity, a belief in moral justice and contempt for the petty rules of law. And it is the flouting of these rules and the rigid conventions of society that so often leads him into trouble.

When Ross returns to his ancestral home, Nampara, he discovers his father's house has fallen into ruin and his inherited land is barren. He is appalled also to discover that villagers living on Poldark land have been left destitute and hungry as a result.

'When we first meet Ross he is in turmoil,' says Aidan Turner, who plays Ross Poldark. 'He went away to war a young, cocky, confident character with a carefree attitude, who was running away from a lot of things. In America he was faced with death on a daily basis and then when he returns to England he doesn't really know who is he is any more.

'When he arrives back in Cornwall everything's changed for him: his father has died, his land is barren, the local tin mines are going through a hard time and laying off workers, leaving the region on its knees, and he's lost Elizabeth, his childhood sweetheart who he expected to marry on his return.

'Ross knows he needs to pick himself up and try and find who he is and where he is in this new world. He's strong – that's what I love about him – he's someone who can get on with things; he doesn't wallow in self-pity or despair. He sees a situation for what it is and drags himself through it. He admires hard-working people and treats people with respect if they earn it – no matter what their position in life. He is an original class warrior!'

CHARLES POLDARK

'It's a poor Cornwall you return to. Taxes sky high, wages in the gutter . . .'

Of Ross's disregard for class and the conventions of society, screenwriter Debbie Horsfield agrees: 'He straddles two different backgrounds. He's a gentleman so he's from the landed gentry but he has huge, not just sympathy, but love for the common man, for his tenants, his miners that he employs. He's in love with a girl who's a gentlewoman's daughter, a girl from his own class, but he ends up marrying his kitchen maid. He has a strong sense of justice without in any way being sanctimonious. He's a rebel and everybody loves a rebel.'

The American War:
Revolution and *Taxation*

The era of the Poldarks is marked by turbulence both at home and abroad. Growing rebellion in the American colonies (initially sparked by opposition to heavy taxes imposed by

Beatie Edney (Prudie): 'Aidan's got charisma and that matinee idol thing – and he's incredibly professional. It must be very daunting: he's in every scene, he has to ride a horse, do love scenes, talk about tin mines, go through grief and all kinds of emotions, and he keeps it all together. There aren't many people who can do that and he's very nice to everybody as well. He works unbelievably long hours and he seems to thrive on it.'

George Washington accepts the surrender of British forces at Yorktown, 1781.

Britain) has, by 1776, led to the Declaration of Independence, all-out war and the sending of thousands of British troops to fight on American soil. Two years later, the French, Spanish and Dutch have allied with America against Britain, turning a colonial uprising into a global conflict.

In the television adaptation of *Poldark*, we first meet our hero Ross in a wooded glade in Virginia in 1781 where, sitting amidst a group of bedraggled soldiers, he is playing cards. Suddenly a musket shot rings out and they are under attack, Ross's opponent falling to the ground, dead. As all hell breaks loose, Ross seizes four muskets and dispatches two attacking soldiers, before receiving a glancing wound to his face from a tomahawk.

The war limps on until 1783, ending in defeat for the British and continued independence for the Americans. Ross returns home a changed man, three years of fighting having worn down much of his youthful swagger. The defeat also reveals the weakness of Britain as a nation without significant allies. And many, like Ross, sympathize with the American cause and its revolutionary ideas of liberty.

Funding such a costly war has a direct effect on the whole country, especially in Cornwall. Servicing the soaring National Debt costs the British government some £9 million a year. As a result, the government introduces a range of taxes, raising duties on such consumables as salt, beer and even candles, much of which weighs heaviest on the poor. This in turn leads to increased poverty, hardship and a rising incidence of social unrest.

With troops overseas, there is little monitoring of the British coast and smuggling is rife. As this illicit trade continues, 'strange whiffs of volcanic unrest' are felt across the Channel, which ultimately lead to revolution in France in 1789 and aristocrats losing their heads. Whilst this doesn't happen in Britain, recurring bread riots and outbreaks of violence leads to an increasing feeling of insecurity and, amongst the propertied classes, an almost universal dread of insurrection.

AIDAN TURNER *is* Ross Poldark

The man behind the unconventional but captivating hero of *Poldark* is Irish actor Aidan Turner. Having starred in *The Hobbit* trilogy, *Being Human* and *Desperate Romantics*, Aidan was thrilled to land the role of Ross Poldark.

He was also immediately taken by the characters of the *Poldark* stories and by the breadth of the role of Ross Poldark in the new adaptation. 'It's fantastic as an actor to have the chance to play such a wide range in one series,' he says. 'Every step of the way there is something new. When I first read Debbie Horsfield's script I knew there was huge scope there with Ross.'

The decision to cast Aidan as Ross was a crucial one for the *Poldark* production team, as Debbie Horsfield explains: 'I loved Aidan in *Desperate Romantics* and *Being Human* and I thought he had that blend of charisma but he was able to play vulnerable

Aidan Turner: 'One of the highlights in filming was riding Seamus, the horse. There's an energy when you deliver dialogue on a horse, it's empowering especially for Ross, he thrives on these kinds of situations, so any time I could get on the horse I would do it.

'Seamus is quite skittish, but he's a real actor's horse as you can rehearse something once and he knows where he's at, the direction he's going in, when he has to stop and reset. We had to change words as he would just set off when we shouted "Action". He was so sharp and always moving and on the go. He and Ross are well suited!'

yet tough. Ross is a man of contradictions and I'd seen that in Aidan's work. Ross is an outsider, he's a rebel and I just thought that Aidan was the person to play him.'

Aidan, who's in his early thirties, had never heard of *Poldark* prior to making the series, 'but when I told my parents I was going to play Ross they nearly had a fit! Apparently the previous 1970s series was popular in Ireland, I guess because people could relate to it – the farming, the scenery, the horses . . . it is continually surprising meeting people who are so excited to hear we are making a new adaptation.'

Ross

*'I can't stay.
I only called to let you know
I've returned. I must trouble
you for a horse, Charles.*

But first, a toast.
To *Elizabeth . . .*

And Francis . . .

May they find happiness together.'

Above: *Director Ed Bazalgette with Aidan Turner. Phil Davis (Jud): 'Aidan brings tremendous swagger to the role, he's quite a dangerous-looking character.'*

Aidan's strong physical presence was also key to his portrayal of Ross, as director Ed Bazalgette remarks: 'Ross Poldark has that raw power and energy. He'll say what he thinks and do what he wants. Those fundamental attributes are things that you could really see Aidan carrying. Aidan also has an extraordinary relationship with the camera and a physicality that makes him incredibly watchable. There's also a fun, mischievous side to him, and a warmth. He's not a stern person in any way, he's just very much a man of the people.'

Eleanor Tomlinson, who plays Demelza, can see why Aidan was chosen for the role, too: 'He gives the character Ross an edge – he makes him unpredictable. And that's interesting with your leading man because sometimes you don't know if you hate him and that for me is fascinating.'

Eleanor Tomlinson as Demelza Carne.

From the outset, Ross is faced with tough decisions and is forced to overcome huge challenges. 'Ross is twenty-three when he comes home and you can see he changes quite fast,' says Aidan Turner. 'When he realizes that Elizabeth is out of the picture, he changes his frame of mind and concentrates more on getting his land back together, looking after his tenants, and resolves to revive the ruined mine on his estate.'

And soon after Ross meets a woman who will change the course of his life, an urchin who he at first takes to be a young boy: Demelza Carne.

'Taking on Demelza as his kitchen maid and understanding how that whole relationship develops is a huge moment for Ross. He doesn't care what people think, but he's taken a huge punt bringing her into the house and having her as a kitchen maid. Eventually he takes charge, doesn't quite know what he's got himself in for but very quickly he realizes he's got to do something about it. Ross just grabs everything by the horns and runs with it!

'He is continually facing something new; his changing relationship with his cousin Francis, his uncle Charles who he has looked up to all his life and who is a rock for him, and the feud with George Warleggan.'

Cornwall

When Ross is confronted with the choice either to remain in Cornwall and cope with the devastation around him or take his uncle's money, move away and start afresh, he decides to stay, knowing that he can make a difference to the people he loves. As he discovers, everything that matters to him is in Cornwall.

Cornwall is at the very heart of *Poldark*, its rugged beauty and wild landscape a constant, powerful presence. In the 1780s, Cornwall is a sparsely populated, far-flung region of Britain jutting dangerously out into the Atlantic Ocean, very much on its own. Its landscape is of wild open moorland, savage cliffs tumbling into angry sea and weather that can in an instant change from swirling sea mists and squally gales to (just occasionally) brilliantly clear skies. Out of this robust and dangerously beautiful terrain emerges our hero Ross Poldark, a character who seemingly embodies the tempestuous nature of Cornwall.

Production designer Catrin Meredydd: 'As soon as you've bought an actor on board Mark Atkinson, the horse master, starts to train them, and when they feel comfortable with a horse they stick with that one throughout. In a funny way the horse often chooses them.'

Aidan Turner: 'They wouldn't let me gallop along the cliff top, for obvious reasons, but I did as much as possible.'

Winston Graham's Cornwall

The inspiration for the *Poldark* novels was drawn from the creator Winston Graham's love of Cornwall; many of the series' storylines were borne out of real events in Cornish history, its characters inspired by the people he had met there.

Graham lived much of his life on the North Cornish coast and during the Second World War worked as a coastguard overlooking the beach at Perranporth. It was during long nights and solitary walks patrolling the beaches that he conceived the *Poldark* novels, with Hendrawna beach based on Perranporth, and Nampara and its surrounding area a composite of several places on the north coast of Cornwall, including the headland of West Pentire. Here he spent much of his time 'watching the flickering colours in the water; the white flash of gulls' wings, angular and sharp, against slanting skies; the sea pinks clinging perpendicularly to the gentler rocks like close-cropped pink beards, the thump of waves forcing their way through a blow hole and turning spume into mist; the welter of wild flowers in the unspoiled fields . . . the endless procession of cloud and sun against the background of wide skies.'

Winston Graham's son Andrew Graham was also very much involved in the making of the television adaptation. From very early on he looked at scripts, was involved in casting and location finding, and was often on set during filming. As he adds: 'There were all sorts of things with which we [Andrew and his wife Peggotty] helped out, from smaller details, such as specifics on the geography of Cornwall, which I know well, to the bigger picture. I kept asking whether things would make sense from my father's point of view. We had a really productive relationship with Mammoth Screen and it was clear right from the start that the production team wanted to create something that was authentic to the novels.'

Director Ed Bazalgette: 'We had a fantastic gift courtesy of nature. In terms of working out how it was going to look, how it was going to feel and what our palette was. Because we had Cornwall itself. Everywhere you look there were inspirational opportunities. Even something simple like a piece of slate, or gorse in the early spring, the vibrant purples and pinks of the heather, even the lichen on the houses you've got this very dynamic limey-electric green. So our mood boards and colour swatches were all informed by the colours of Cornwall.'

For the television adaptation, Cornwall provided a crucial backdrop and setting, with the filming of the series largely based in or around the North Cornish coast. 'Cornwall is a massive part of the book and our adaptation,' says executive producer Karen Thrussell. 'Nowhere else looks like it: the huge skies, four-seasons-in-one-day climate, the quality of light, its rugged beauty scarred with mines, the powerful surging sea and the wind-beaten moors. The elemental passion of the landscape and changeable nature of the place have echoes of Ross Poldark's personality.'

The cast also relished their time filming in Cornwall, not least Aidan Turner: 'It was simply stunning, we had the best weather there over the summer. We filmed at so many gorgeous locations but the weather really made it work. People know *Poldark* so well down there and are proud of it so we were welcomed all the time. It was surprising getting fans turning

In the first part of the eighteenth century, tin mining had boomed in Cornwall (see page 46). By the end of the century, however, falling prices in tin and copper led to a drop in wages and the closure of many mines. These abandoned mines peppered and scarred much of the Cornish landscape, whilst its communities sank into deprivation and uncertainty.
Right: *Executive producers Karen Thrussell and Damien Timmer.*

War hero

The inspiration for Ross's physical appearance came from a chance acquaintance Winston Graham made in a railway station just after the Second World War. A young flying officer, with a couple of ribs and a leg broken and bearing a scratch to his face, sat opposite him. To Graham he seemed withdrawn but pleasant,

while also purposeful with 'a sort of high-strung disquiet'. On seeing him, the novelist immediately knew that this man was to be the model for his hero. Ross's own scar, inflicted dangerously close to his eye, provides a constant reminder of the war and his near brush with death.

The first *Poldark* novel was published in 1945, just as British troops were returning from the Second World War. Many came back to confront shattered homes, their families and loved ones torn apart. Ross Poldark similarly returns from fighting overseas to discover his father dead, and his house, means of livelihood and former love in ruins.

up to the set and people travelling to show their support and see what was going on. It reminded me of home in Ireland, and it was great to be able to film there so much.'

Eleanor Tomlinson was similarly enchanted by the county: 'So much of it came alive when we were filming in Cornwall and everyone found their character in the outdoors, particularly with Demelza as she is very connected to the landscape.' Heida Reed, who played Elizabeth, also instantly loved the wide-open spaces of Cornwall: 'I felt like when we were down in Cornwall the whole story came together in my head. The landscape is so vital in the storytelling and when we were there it all fitted together. That Cornish vista is such a part of the story and people's inner lives and it is an incredible place.'

ELIZABETH (to Ross)

'Everything that matters to you is in Cornwall.'

HEIDA REED *is* Elizabeth Chynoweth

Heida Reed plays Ross's childhood sweetheart Elizabeth Chynoweth. Whilst Ross endures the miseries of war, he clings to the memories of Elizabeth, cherishing the ring she has given him as a memento of their love. He is away, however, for a long three years and rumours circulate about his death. Convinced that this is the case, Elizabeth agrees to marry Ross's cousin and old friend Francis Poldark.

Ross's unexpected return shocks Elizabeth to her very core and she is clearly tormented by her still-deep feelings for Ross. All too aware of her elevated standing in society, however, she attempts to bury those feelings and remain true to her prospective husband, a pretence that soon wears away at her sham of a marriage.

'I think Elizabeth is very much a lady of her time, trapped in her own world,' says Heida Reed. 'It is important for Elizabeth to know her place in society and be respected by those around her. She could follow her heart more but she feels morally she must do the right thing even if she suffers for it. Elizabeth never voices regret but I think her predicament will strike a chord with people today.

'It was an awful miscommunication and Elizabeth is the type of person who will do the right thing and stick with her decision because that is what she thinks a good person does – and that still stands in modern society.'

Soon after their wedding, Francis begins to absent himself from the family home, his behaviour spiralling out of control. Throughout it all Elizabeth maintains composure and strength, whilst also showing a real generosity of spirit by welcoming Ross's new wife Demelza into her home. Whilst Ross's attachment to Demelza deepens, he still clearly retains feelings for his first love Elizabeth, a woman whose elegance, social standing and deportment make her the polar opposite of the untamed Demelza.

ROSS
'Elizabeth was born to be admired.'

DEMELZA
'An' I was born to pull turnips?'

Having grown up in Iceland and still only twenty-six, Heida Reed wasn't aware of the *Poldark* phenomenon before taking on the role but she instantly loved the stories and the complex way the characters develop through the series.

She particularly enjoyed filming in Cornwall, although it wasn't all plain sailing, as she explains: 'I had never ridden a horse before so went to the horse master for lessons before we started filming. I learnt to ride side-saddle, which was definitely the most challenging and exciting thing I had to do.

'Every time I sat on a horse I used to think he would throw me off and I would die! It was exhilarating and I felt so proud of myself for getting through it. I actually enjoyed riding side-saddle – I found it more comfortable than sitting astride.'

Whilst Heida is without doubt a natural beauty, a huge amount of work also went into creating Elizabeth's look. Heida jokes that she was the most high-maintenance actor in *Poldark*!

'I was definitely more time-consuming than even Aidan Turner! I was never done with fittings, the costume department were meticulous and a lot of my fabrics had to be dyed again and again, taken up or down a shade, so they matched my skin tone.

'Elizabeth is a very glamorous character but she's still quite pragmatic. There weren't all the lace details you see in so many of these period dramas. Over the four years that the series spans, Elizabeth goes through phases and becomes more natural as time moves on as she doesn't have the time and probably doesn't care as much.'

Nonetheless, the result is quite simply stunning, creating a female character who captivates and beguiles many of those around her, not least her first love, Ross, who is still instinctively drawn to her charm and dazzling beauty.

George III *and the* Prince of Wales

The British monarch George III is blamed for the defeat of the American War of Independence and faces a difficult time with his ministers. In 1783, however, the talented and supportive politician William Pitt the Younger becomes Prime Minister, and will remain in power until 1801. In 1788 the King falls ill with his first bout of 'madness'. His withdrawal from public life triggers a political crisis, with the Whigs (the main opponents to the Tories and a reforming, constitutional party), led by Charles James Fox, keen for the Prince of Wales, the king's oldest son and a Whig supporter, to become Regent. The dissolute Prince of Wales is vastly unpopular, but, thankfully, by April 1789 the King has recovered and returns to his royal duties, thereby ending the crisis (for the time being).

George III, Queen Charlotte and their six eldest children *by Johann Zoffany, 1770.*

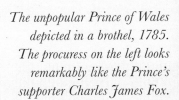

The unpopular Prince of Wales depicted in a brothel, 1785. The procuress on the left looks remarkably like the Prince's supporter Charles James Fox.

CHAPTER TWO

The closure of a local mine, Wheal Reath, puts hundreds of miners out of work and leaves them desperately poor. With Nampara now repaired, Ross employs Jim Carter as a farm hand and looks to resurrect his family's mine, Wheal Leisure. Ross's work-shy servants Jud and Prudie grumble about the arrival of Demelza as kitchen maid at Nampara. During a ball at the Assembly Rooms, Francis's sister Verity meets and falls madly in love with Captain Andrew Blamey. The captain, however, has a scandalous past, and her father forbids her from seeing him. Francis challenges Blamey to an ill-fated duel, after which the captain leaves and Ross saves Francis's life.

R oss's banker and friend Harris Pascoe advises Ross against opening a new mine, believing he won't be able to find speculators in the current climate. With the help of mine captain Henshawe and willing investor Horace Treneglos, Ross manages to convince Pascoe that Wheal Leisure is a viable business and sets about preparing for its opening.

ROSS POLDARK

'The rewards could be considerable but so are the risks. But if you like a wager – and which of us here doesn't? Then I'd sooner gamble on a vein of copper and the sweat of fifty men than on the turn of a card.'

Cornish Mining

In the first part of the eighteenth century, the Poldarks did very well out of the great Grambler mine and the smaller Wheal Leisure and Wheal Grace mines. Since the Romans invaded Britain, Cornwall had been famous for its tin and a vast wealth of minerals beneath its surface, particularly in the west of the county where the Poldark estates lie. Great landowners – such as the real-life Godolphins and Bassets of Tehidy – thus began to work the land for its metals, which drew into the area a large number of migrant workers and their families. For the next two centuries the history of Cornwall was the history of mining, with many reliant on the industry for their livelihood.

In the 1770s and 1780s, however, the price of tin and copper fell, caused by the national economic depression, increasing competition from Welsh mines and the smelting companies illegally pushing the prices down further to maximize their profits. Miners' wages, which were determined by the price of ore, fell too and mines like Wheal Leisure were eventually forced to close. To reopen any mine during this difficult period was therefore deemed a hazardous enterprise, of considerable risk to its investors (known as 'adventurers'). Learning of Ross's intention to reopen Wheal Leisure, his drunkard servant, Jud, warns of the foolhardiness of such a venture, claiming that the untimely death of Ross's own father was because 'mining did fer 'im'.

The closure of so many mines nonetheless opened up opportunities for others, Ross reminding potential investors that the recent closure of Wheal Reath should result in a rise of prices. (In reality, good times were only just ahead as demand from new markets led to a rise in copper prices in the 1790s, peaking in 1805, when Cornwall had become the greatest producer of copper in the world.)

In Ross's father's day, we are told, Wheal Leisure had been worked for surface tin only but from samples taken from the mine, Ross knows there are also definite signs of copper. Usually large

Wheal Owles mine near Botallack was recreated into Ross's Wheal Leisure mine. Production designer Catrin Meredydd: 'We clad onto an existing mine engine house at Wheal Owles. We copied a lot of the original designs for the equipment used by the bal-maidens, the women and children working above ground. We also built a large horse-whim, which was quite a big piece of equipment to make practical [so that it would work].'

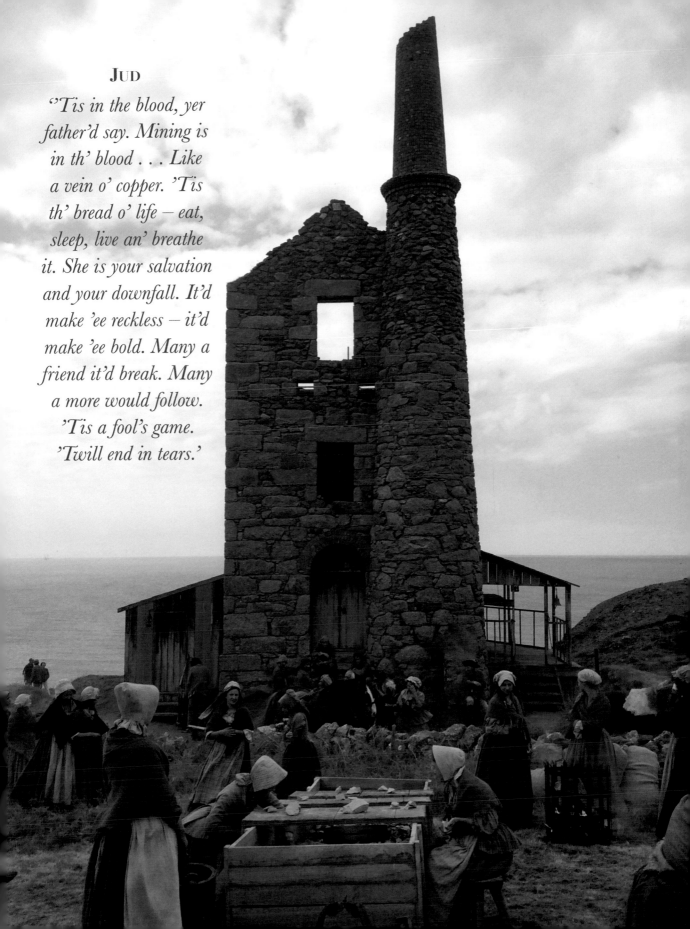

JUD

''Tis in the blood, yer father'd say. Mining is in th' blood . . . Like a vein o' copper. 'Tis th' bread o' life — eat, sleep, live an' breathe it. She is your salvation and your downfall. It'd make 'ee reckless — it'd make 'ee bold. Many a friend it'd break. Many a more would follow. 'Tis a fool's game. 'Twill end in tears.'

lodes or veins of copper ore are found deep underground and miners have to dig tunnels and sink shafts. Once Wheal Leisure is opened, they immediately hit ironstone, which is a good indication of copper, but getting at it requires the use of explosives and additional funds for gunpowder.

Once copper ore was found, miners like Zacky Martin and Mark Daniel, known as 'tributers', mined the rock and chose the best lode to send to the surface. Ore was loaded onto wheelbarrows or dragged on trays, then placed in iron buckets (kibbles) and hoisted by horses to the surface.

On the surface and under the direction of 'grass captains', the ore was 'dressed', broken into small pieces by women

Above: *Ross consults with his mine captain, Mr Henshawe.*
Right: *The bal-maidens at work, with the horse-whim in the background.*

Andrew Graham: 'My father really came to know the people and many voices of Cornwall. He learned about their lives as farmers, fishermen, miners, and shop-keepers as it had been in their fathers' and grandfathers' times. It is from these people that many of the characters in Poldark *draw breath and life. He would have been totally delighted to see the characters he so loved coming to life yet again on the small screen.'*

('bal-maidens') with long-handled hammers, ground into powder by stamping-mills using water power and washed by children to remove all waste material. It was then sent for smelting (see page 125).

Our hero Ross, as the purser of the mine, manages its finances, making sure it has enough money to keep going. As in *Poldark*, mines were run on capitalist lines, with accounts presented at regular meetings, often at inns such as the Red Lion, where adventurers subscribed further capital or received profits divided amongst them. Mining operations were directed by experienced foremen known as 'bal-captains', and tributers' wages varied with the pitch, and location and prosperity of the mines. For the majority of those working either in the mines or on the surface, hours were long, conditions dismal and pay, although often higher than those of farm labourers, still pitifully low.

Above (left to right): *Mark Daniel (Matthew Wilson), Jim Carter (Alexander Arnold), Zacky Martin (Tristan Sturrock) and Paul Daniel (Ed Browning).*
Left: *Jim Carter's sweetheart Jinny (Gracee O'Brien).*
Right: *A contemporary account by the physician George Lipscomb (1773–1846) describes the harsh realities of mining in Cornwall.*

George Lipscomb, *A Journey into Cornwall*, 1799

The shafts where the miners descend and by which the ore is raised to the surface are scattered over an extent of sterile country; whose dreary appearance and the sallow faces of the miners concur to awaken the most dismal and gloomy ideas. But, though rugged the surface, the interior is fraught with the richest treasures. . . . Though withered the complexion and miserable their appearance, by [the miners'] labours are the finest works of art brought to perfection and their industry is a strong pillar of the state.

The descent into the mine is performed by means of ladders placed almost perpendicularly so that it is a very dangerous passage. You are furnished with a suit of clothes . . . and are accompanied by a guide who carries a light before you. The damps of these subterraneous caverns are sometimes so baneful and offensive that the stranger, unaccustomed to expeditions of this nature, is not infrequently tempted to recede rather than subject himself to their noxious effects. We descended more than forty ladders, slippery with humidity and worn out by the feet of the labourers, before we reached the deepest part of the mine.

Those who dig in these wretched dismal excavations are under the necessity of breathing so much impure air that their health is speedily injured and they die, at an early period, hectic [feverish] or paralytic.

The wages paid for labour are, however, so considerable, that workmen are always to be met with, ready to sacrifice their health and strength in these dark and gloomy mansions.

The labourers employed in the mines are usually exchanged at short intervals, it being necessary to their health and indeed to their very existence, that they should emerge from the deleterious humidity of these caverns and breathe a purer air.

The Miners seem to be and indeed are a race of men distinct from the common class of British subjects; they are governed by laws and customs almost exclusively their own; and wild as their native rocks, and rugged as the hordes of Africa they are separated from the manners of modern improvement and resemble the primitive possessors of an uncultivated soil rather than kindred brethren of a great and enlightened nation. . . . Remote from the advantageous influence of a Court, unbiased by ministerial intrigues, subject to every hardship . . . the miners are loyal to their King.

The engine houses of Wheal Owles (left), which was recreated into Wheal Leisure for Poldark, *and Wheal Edward (right) on the South West Coast Path, Cornwall.*

William Pryce, *Mineralogia Cornubiensis*, 1778

(including 'an explanation of the cornu-technical terms and idioms of the tinners')

Adventure. *A mine in working is so called, and so is the affair of being concerned in a mine, as it is usual to say, "A person is about to take up an Adventure".*

Adventurers. *Are those persons concerned in a Mine who have Doles, shares, or parts thereof. Out-Adventurers are those who contribute their quotas of the charge, but do not give a daily attendance. But In-Adventurers are such who have Doles and also work in or attend the affairs of the Mine for wages.*

Axletree. *A thick piece of timber in form of a cylinder with a large rope wound about it, and with which they bring up the work or Ore, and usually let the men descend and come up.*

Bal. *A shovel or a place of digging. When many people are employed in a Mine of note, in sorting the Ore, where it is brought to grass, then they stile this place where the concourse of people meet and work by the name of the Bal.*

Bottom captain. *A superintendent over the Miners in the Bottoms [the deepest part of the mine].*

Captain. *An experienced Miner, who directs and oversees the workmen and business of the Mine.*

Dole – or Dol. *Any part or share of the Adventure.*

Lord of the Land. *The person in whose land the Mine is.*

Moorhouse. *A hovel built with turf for workmen to change clothes in.*

Set. *A set is the ground granted to a company of Adventurers.*

Slocking stone. *A tempting, inducing, or rich stone of Ore. Some Miners produce good stones of Ore, which induce the concerned to proceed, until they expend much money perhaps, and at last find the Mine good for nothing; so, likewise, there have been some instances of Miners who have deceived their employers by bringing them Slocking stones from other Mines, pretending they were found in the Mine they worked in.*

Slottere. *Dirty, slovenly muddy.*

Small men/fairies. *The Miners are sometimes persuaded that they hear a pick at work under-ground, as if some invisible spirit was at work underneath or near them. This noise, I suppose, proceeds from the running or falling of waters through the crevices and apertures of the earth. The opinion the Miners have of its being a good omen encourages them to follow or work to it; so that it has more than once occasioned some lucky discovery.*

Tinners. *All Cornish miners.*

RUBY BENTALL *is* Verity Poldark

A character who is thrilled to see Ross return to Cornwall is his cousin and old friend Verity Poldark. Unmarried at twenty-five, the kind, modest daughter of Charles Poldark seems destined to live life as a spinster, attending to the needs of her family and household.

The monotony of her existence, however, is considerably lightened by Ross's return, as Ruby Bentall, who plays Verity, explains: 'When Ross arrives home unexpectedly from the war she hasn't got any other thought in her head apart from, "He's alive!" While everyone else around the table is thinking about how his return will complicate things, Verity's the only one that just has this pure happiness to see him. They have a better relationship than she has with her brother Francis so for her it's like her brother coming home.'

One of the most straightforward members of the Poldark family, Verity is good-natured and clearly fond of Ross, who, unlike her family, treats her more as an equal. 'She's got a massive heart and is very kind and caring,' Ruby says. 'She gets treated quite poorly by her family, who don't seem to recognize what a great person she is and take advantage of her kindness. But she does also have great strength at times.'

In a society in which marriage remained the prime objective of young women, particularly amongst the landed gentry, Verity's prospects seem bleak. Living in Cornwall where there is a limited choice of prospective husbands, and without the beauty and confidence to sell herself, Verity is largely doomed to a life of looking after her father, brother and servants of the household.

Meeting and falling in love with Captain Blamey finally gives Verity the opportunity to escape the drudgery of her existence. Her hopes however are soon dashed when we learn of Captain Blamey's violent and drunkard past: in an alcohol-fuelled

argument his wife was accidentally killed. Verity's father and her brother Francis immediately forbid the marriage, although we suspect it's more to protect the Poldark name than out of any real concern for Verity's welfare or happiness.

When Ross marries Demelza, Verity is the first to congratulate him and quickly befriends Demelza, welcoming her into the family. As Ruby puts it: 'That's just her personality – she's not quick to judge, she'll let someone talk, she'll listen and make up her own mind. She's just a very reasonable person. She loves Ross and wants to see what Demelza's like and understand why he likes her. Verity is very rational and quick-tempered, and is much cleverer than her dad and her brother in that way, even though she is less educated.

'I really enjoyed the scenes where Verity teaches Demelza about etiquette and how to dance. Once she gets to know Demelza and understands that she needs help, she is there to provide it. It's in her kind nature to do that, she enjoys helping people. In the end it turns out that Demelza helps her as much as she helps Demelza, so they get quite close and have a really nice relationship.'

Despite having appeared in other period dramas, including the BBC's adaptation of *Lark Rise to Candleford* and *Lost in Austen*, there were elements of Verity's character that Ruby found challenging, not least wearing a corset: 'You can see why women couldn't do anything in those days because everything was such hard work – walking upstairs, lying down, eating! You look nice but it is so impractical.'

Gentlewomen of the period were required to ride side-saddle, a skill that Ruby also found tricky to master: 'You have no support, you can't grip with your legs as they are just lying there! How women used to go hunting and jumping I don't know.'

However, like many of the cast and crew, Ruby thoroughly enjoyed her time in Cornwall: 'I rode a lot as a kid but have never ridden for a job and there was one point when Aidan and I were on our horses waiting for a shot to be set up, looking over a cliff with the sun shining on clear water and it was the most beautiful place in the world.'

Right: *Captain Blamey is tortured by his past. He loves Verity but Francis Poldark and his father, Charles, want to have nothing to do with him because of the violent death of his first wife.*

Poldark Women

The female characters of Demelza, Elizabeth and Verity illustrate well the complexities and challenges of women's lives during the Georgian period. Without any means to support themselves, many women, like Elizabeth, would have chosen the security of a well-matched marriage over life as a single woman. Francis, a young, attractive heir to a substantial estate, is on paper the perfect choice for Elizabeth. Ross, a risk-taker with an unpredictable disregard for the social norms, would have been a far more dangerous prospect for a gentlewoman like Elizabeth.

This sensible marriage, nonetheless, descends into misery as Francis squanders his inheritance and takes up with prostitutes, brushing off his own infidelity as a pursuit common to all gentlemen. As a result, Elizabeth is forced to tolerate his indiscretions, as was typical in a society in which the moral expectations of men and women contrasted greatly. The social contract between husbands and wives is summed up by the contemporary Dr Johnson: 'The chastity of women is of importance, as all property depends on it.' By contrast, 'between man and wife, a husband's infidelity is nothing . . . Wise married women don't trouble themselves about infidelity in their husbands . . .'

Verity, who is entirely dependent on the men in her family, shows what little power unmarried women had at the time. She can't work and with limited prospect of marriage, her only means of security is to be indispensable at home, her life devoted

Pamela is Married by Joseph Highmore. The bestselling novel of its time, Pamela: or Virtue Rewarded *tells the story of a beautiful fifteen-year-old maid whose upper-class master eventually marries her.*

to the caring of others. Added to that, once her brother marries, Elizabeth immediately outranks Verity as mistress of the house, cementing further her subservient role in the household.

Demelza, who is born of lower stock, is freer with her nature and emotions, but living with her father she too suffers at the behest of a cruel and drunken man. It is only by Ross taking on her father that she finally escapes his clutches, although the subsequent marriage between Demelza, a kitchen maid, and a gentleman like Ross would have been largely unthinkable for many Georgians (although it was an escapist fantasy that made Samuel Richardson's *Pamela* a bestseller). True to his devil-may-care character, however, Ross defies all convention and marries his kitchen maid, a turn of events that, whilst not quite grounded in history, certainly adds to the epic romance of the series.

KYLE SOLLER *is* Francis Poldark

Playing Verity's brother Francis is American actor Kyle Soller.
A graduate of RADA in London, before *Poldark* Kyle appeared
in various West End theatre productions as well as the BBC
comedy *Bad Education*.

Kyle was immediately attracted to the character of Francis
Poldark, in particular the journey he takes from a fresh-faced
young man besotted with his soon-to-be wife Elizabeth to an
absentee husband who drinks heavily, commits adultery and
gambles away his inheritance.

'I think he's perhaps more flawed than most but he has a
huge self-confidence issue and is constantly living in the shadow
of his cousin Ross,' explains Kyle. 'He has an overbearing father
who he can never please and he feels he doesn't have a place in
life. He doesn't want to go into mining as he's not up to handling
the business side and he can't be the swashbuckling hero.

'Francis's relationship with his father Charles is awkward and
you get the feeling that his father would have preferred to have
had a child like Ross, who's very strong and outgoing. Francis
loves his father and has a lot of respect for him but at the same
time, he's never been good enough so he's pretty hard on himself.'

To Francis, family honour is of real importance, which
Kyle thinks is one of his better qualities. 'The problem is when
his family honour is at stake he reacts irrationally, almost like
a child, and that's another one of his downfalls; he can be
extremely brash and impetuous. But the seed of that emotion
and reaction is correct – he wants the best for everyone,
especially his sister.'

Growing up, Ross and Francis formed a close friendship.
'Ross was the guy that always fought Francis's battles and
was always there for him,' says Kyle. 'Francis has never really
worked a day in his life, he's never had to stand up for himself
really so I guess the relationship is one of dependency. When
Ross comes back, that all just gets completely thrown out of

FRANCIS

*'Damn Ross!
Damn his
scheming. He
has married
my sister to
a wife beater
and he has
disgraced the
family name. If
he cares so little
for my interest
why should I
care for his?'*

Francis with his father Charles (played by Warren Clarke). As a son, Francis is a disappointment to his father.

kilter and this really interesting love triangle develops and that kick-starts his decline.'

On the worsening relationship between Ross and Francis, Aidan Turner adds: 'Francis has changed a lot since Ross has left. He has become more of a man and befriended a lot of people that Ross wouldn't have time for, like the Warleggans, the bankers and some of the less desirable people around the town. So the relationship with Francis is strained.'

Soon after Ross returns from America, he and Francis end up arguing while they are in a mineshaft, after which Francis falls in open water and almost drowns before Ross – after a split second of indecision – rescues him. Filming the scene was challenging for Kyle: 'Francis really gets himself into some sticky situations that would be a big test for anyone. The scene in the mineshaft was really scary on an acting level. Being down in the mineshaft with open water, in a situation where someone is really angry at you and wanting to punch you in the face, it was scary.'

Kyle enjoyed filming the duelling scene, when Francis and Captain Blamey fight it out over Verity. 'The duel, with a man threatening to take his sister away, was so much fun as we got to use actual pistols they would have used at the time – there was a really amazing technical team that helped us out.'

Duelling – *A Code of* Honour

The duel between Francis and Captain Blamey occurs suddenly and without warning, with Francis intent on preserving the family honour of the Poldarks and still fuming about Ross's betrayal. Amongst the upper classes, the custom of settling arguments by duels was a familiar practice, and one that lasted well into the nineteenth century. They were fought with either pistols or swords, with firearms beginning to gain favour in this period. More often than not, duels were based on a code of honour, motivated by the participants' desire not so much to kill their opponents but to show their willingness to risk their lives to restore their honour.

Many disapproved of the practice, whereas others felt it helped to encourage good manners amongst gentlemen. (Far better to raise one's hat and avoid argument than risk being shot in a duel.) Politicians of the day were also known to duel, with Winston Graham basing some of the duels in the novels on those of the radical politician John Wilkes, who duelled twice with Lord Talbot and the Secretary of the Treasury, Mr Martin. In 1798, even the Prime Minister, Pitt the Younger, exchanged shots with leading Whig George Tierney, after Tierney accused Pitt of putting the defences of the country in danger. In 1765, Lord Byron (great-uncle of the poet) famously duelled with a Mr Chaworth at the Star and Garter tavern in London, resulting in Byron stabbing his opponent in the stomach.

1763: Samuel Martin MP, a supporter of George III, has just shot and wounded John Wilkes, the radical libertarian. The bullet bounced off Wilkes's waistcoat buttons and lodged in his groin. He eventually recovered, his reputation as a man of honour much enhanced.

FRANCIS
*'I will have
satisfaction!'*

CHAPTER THREE

Wheal Leisure is opened and Ross offers a local young couple, Jim and Jinny, a rent-free cottage so they can marry. Elizabeth gives birth to a boy, Geoffrey Charles, but during the christening party Charles Poldark has a heart attack. Jim is caught poaching. Ross speaks for him at the trial but cannot restrain himself from criticizing the court. Jim is sentenced to prison. Back at Nampara, furious with himself for his failure to save Jim, Ross allows himself to be seduced by Demelza. In defiance of his class, he marries her.

ELEANOR TOMLINSON *is* Demelza Carne

One of the most extraordinary characters in *Poldark* is Demelza. When we first meet her she is dressed like an urchin boy, scrapping on a Truro street in a bid to rescue her beloved dog, Garrick. Ross rescues her from the fray and takes her to Nampara where, to the disgruntlement of his long-term servants Jud and Prudie, he employs her as a kitchen maid. There she proves her mettle, works hard and eventually captures both Ross's attention and his heart. From stray waif to the wife of a Poldark, it's an incredible journey, one that has captivated readers and television audiences alike.

Twenty-two-year-old British actress Eleanor Tomlinson, who plays Demelza, was similarly intrigued by the character and admits that she

ROSS

'This is Demelza. She's to help in the kitchen.'

JUD

'Pickin' up brats'll bring 'ee no end o' trouble.'

was prepared to do whatever she could to get the role. Having appeared in films and television series like *Jack and the Giant Slayer* and *The White Queen*, Eleanor was also keen for a new challenge and to try out for a very different role from the more lofty parts she'd played in other period dramas.

'I wanted to really show the director and producers that I could transform myself for this vastly different role. I borrowed my brother's clothes and went into the audition and tried to stay in character as much as possible as they've never seen that side of me. Normally when you audition for leading lady roles, or ones like Elizabeth, you're much more talkative and polite, and you dress nicely. But with Demelza, she needed to have that rougher edge.

'She is extremely resilient, and has this streetwise edge to her but she never becomes too hard. She has to be vastly different to Elizabeth but you still have to love her, so for me that was really interesting to play. Female roles as strong as this don't come around very often.'

Above: *Demelza with her dog Garrick. Production designer Catrin Meredydd: 'As soon as we began, Gill Raddings, our animal-handler, offered up a few dogs. It's not really an art-department decision, but it has to perform, be consistent, and be available for the time we need. I think we chose a good dog!'*

Right: *Eleanor Tomlinson: 'Demelza is just very true and honest, and she wears her heart on her sleeve. She doesn't know etiquette and she's come from nothing. She's so innocent, a breath of fresh air.'*

Eleanor: 'I wanted Demelza to have an unkempt look about her. I didn't want her to look pretty, I just wanted her to be real. I insisted that her hair was red and all over the place, all curly, matted and messy. I felt that was just her – she's wild and I wanted Demelza to be the complete opposite of Elizabeth but still be beautiful in her own way.'
Right: *Beatie Edney (Prudie) takes a selfie with Eleanor.*

The relationship between Ross and Demelza is a key dramatic element of the *Poldark* stories. It begins with a simple act of charity, as Aidan Turner explains: 'Ross's relationship with Demelza is ever-changing. The first time he meets her he thinks she's a boy! He helps her out on a spontaneous whim – there isn't any hidden agenda there, he just thinks he can help out this person. She has it tough and has this rebellious streak and he feels he can make her life better. And obviously then the relationship gains momentum into something else but I don't think either of them saw it coming.'

As Ross gets to know Demelza, he begins to warm to her. 'Demelza has a positive energy,' continues Aidan, 'and she's fun and cheeky and I think he recognizes that outsider thing. She's the opposite of Elizabeth, and rough around the edges but there's a real honesty to Demelza that Ross appreciates. In so much of his life he sees people who aren't honest, who put on a facade and try to be something they're not. With Demelza, she is what she is and she doesn't apologize for it. I think that's attractive to Ross.'

VERITY

'You were always fond of flowers, weren't you? I remember Ross telling me that once.'

(From the novel *Ross Poldark*)

The romance that develops between Ross and Demelza is tempestuous, largely because they share so many traits, as Eleanor comments: 'They're in fact really similar and can both be difficult if they want to be, but they make it work. It's a very real relationship.'

As the story unfolds, Ross's cousin Verity becomes a great friend and mentor to Demelza, giving her much-needed support and lessons on how to act as a lady. At the same time, Demelza feels great sorrow for Verity, trapped at home at Trenwith and unable to pursue her love affair with Captain Blamey. Demelza, unrestrained by the usual inhibitions of the gentry, refuses to accept the situation and engineers a meeting between the two, which, happily for Verity, ends in her eventual elopement.

Another curious relationship to develop is that between Demelza and Ross's former sweetheart, Elizabeth. 'You want

REVEREND ODGERS

'I wonder you don't think of marriage, Captain Poldark?'

ROSS

'I dare say I shall in due course.'

them to hate each other,' says Eleanor. 'You're never friends with the ex-girlfriend! But Elizabeth is just perfect and Demelza can only aspire to be like her not only because she's so beautiful and just oozes this elegance but also because she's captured Ross's heart and she always has it and never loses it, and that's something Demelza has to accept. He loves them both but very differently. At first they hate each other and then they realize they both love the same man and he loves them both – but I get him!'

Whilst Eleanor was aware of the original television series of *Poldark*, she was keen to make the character of Demelza her own. 'There's a fearlessness in the way she plays Demelza,' says director Ed Bazalgette. 'Demelza is so blunt, matter-of-fact, she just lives her life, and I think Eleanor was able to tap into that brilliantly. Eleanor was willing to push herself, not be in her comfort zone and she was really up for exploring the character.'

Aidan Turner similarly enjoyed working with his on-screen lover and wife. 'When I read the scripts, I thought, I hope I get on with this girl and she gets on with me and I hope we work well together. But she's amazing and such a great actor. And again her temperament is incredible, she's quite calm and we can work things out quickly, we almost have a shorthand. We know when someone isn't happy with something. It just works. And she's really attractive and it's not hard to fall in love with her!'

One of the hardest elements of the role for Eleanor was the Cornish accent. 'It was very hard, and being from East Yorkshire I had never really ventured to Cornwall as a kid so that was a continual experience for me as well. I worked very hard with the voice coach who was fantastic and so helpful. With Demelza's accent, she never loses it but she tames it a little bit – I was anxious that she never totally becomes a lady, she is never like Elizabeth and I wanted to keep that trueness to her roots.

'The accent is hard to master and the Cornish people are so passionate about *Poldark*, they're going to be listening for the accent and want it to be perfect. I learnt about how their jaws were a lot tighter because of the wind, and living so close to the sea, the salt makes you speak in a different way. They clench their jaw tightly so you get a completely different sound. One of the main things I found was that the language is like Old English, they use words we haven't even heard nowadays.'

Sweet Demelza

Winston Graham came up with the unusual name of Demelza after seeing it on a signpost on Goss Moor, Cornwall between Roche and Bodmin. Demelza turned out to be a small hamlet (as it is now), but it provided Graham with not only the name of his main character but also, rather magically, the inspiration for her identity, which up to that point had remained elusive. According to an eighteenth-century book on the Cornish language, De means thee or thy, and Melza means honey or sweetness: 'Thy sweetness', therefore, a likely and somewhat fitting meaning for Demelza.

ROBIN ELLIS *is* Reverend Halse

Tensions run high when Jim Carter is sentenced to two years in prison after he is caught poaching. The unsympathetic magistrate who presides over the trial, Reverend Halse, is played by none other than Robin Ellis, who starred as Ross Poldark in the BBC's first television adaptation in the 1970s.

'Very early on in the development of the series Robin Ellis got in touch to offer his good wishes for our success,' says screenwriter Debbie Horsfield. 'I've also been a huge admirer of his work both in TV and theatre, so the idea of finding a role for him was something we were really keen to do. He has a key role in two episodes – and needless to say he was absolutely brilliant.'

The original *Poldark* series, first broadcast in the autumn of 1975, was a huge success for the BBC, with Robin Ellis sending many hearts racing across the nation. This time around the production team was keen to provide an entirely fresh adaptation of the classic novels, rather than a re-make. 'I opted not to watch the 1970s version on DVD until I'd written over half the series,' says Debbie. 'It was interesting to see how much our version, based directly on the novels, differs from the '70s adaptation – although certain key elements appear in both.'

Filming the original series of *Poldark* was life-changing for Robin Ellis, as he explains: 'I'd done a lot of television before *Poldark* but I hadn't done a popular series on BBC 1 so that was a new experience and responsibility. But I had to say it had only a positive effect on my life and was an absolute joy.'

Executive producer Karen Thrussell admits that they were all slightly in awe of Robin Ellis when they met him. But they soon found him incredibly gracious and supportive of the new series. As Robin Ellis says, 'It's been forty years, so why not? There's a whole generation that's never even heard of *Poldark*. And I think the time is right. And the stories are still wonderful.'

ROSS (to Reverend Halse at the trial) *'Then the law is savage and you interpret it without charity! The book from which you preach says that man shall not live by bread alone. These days you're asking him to live without even that!'*

Keen to involve Robin in the new series, the production team offered him the cameo part of Reverend Halse, an offer he couldn't refuse. 'It's quite fun,' says Karen Thrussell, 'because he has lots of scenes with the new Ross Poldark, playing a crusty old judge and they have a couple of dramatic stand-offs.'

'I was thrilled at the idea of coming back to play a small part,' says Robin. 'Reverend Halse is a nasty piece of work, part of the establishment, and one of the gentry that Ross despises. It was a totally new experience to play this sort of character and one I relished.

'As a justice of the peace as well as man of the cloth, Ross first comes into conflict with Reverend Halse when I sentence poor Jim Carter to two years in jail. Ross very rightly gets angry about that. In fact I remember playing the scene when I was Ross Poldark, so it was a curious experience!'

Aidan Turner also remembers it well: 'It was quite a high-octane scene and a lot of it is me shouting at Robin and then storming out of the court room to a round of applause from the locals. I remember after the first take I walked back in and I was quite nervous and there's Robin Ellis and he's sitting there in his gown and cap and looking like a judge. He lowered his glasses and gave me a wink and a thumbs-up and I thought I've been judged by the old Ross Poldark and he gave me a thumbs up – it was such a vote of confidence!'

The second time Ross and Reverend Halse meet is at the gaming-tables of a Warleggan party. Ross, who has been drinking and is still very angry about Jim Carter, cannot help but give Halse a piece of his mind. 'Have you ever been in jail, sir? It's surprising the stench that thirty or forty of God's creatures can give off when confined to a squalid pit for months on end without drains, water or a physician's care . . .' – after which Reverend Halse gets up and stalks out. 'So it's a nice conceit,' says Ellis, 'that the new Ross Poldark sees the old one off the scene!'

Jim Carter in the dock before Reverend Halse.

Before the new series aired, Robin was confident that it would be a success: 'I've always said that it's the stories, the characters and the books of Winston Graham that really anchor the whole thing. New audiences will love the characters, who live their lives passionately. They go through very hard times; it's a three-dimensional story set in the eighteenth century. People will just lap it up.'

ROSS
'You know what people say of us?'

DEMELZA
'Yes.'

ROSS
'If we behave like this, it will be true.'

DEMELZA
'Then let it be true.'

Rich Men Rule *the* Law

Winston Graham, who used real lives and events from the
eighteenth century to inspire so many elements of the *Poldark*
storyline, based the arrest of Jim Carter, his imprisonment
in Bodmin Gaol, fever and death on a case described by the
Methodist preacher John Wesley (1703–91). The deplorable
conditions of Launceston Gaol were similarly based on those
described in the prison reformer John Howard's *State of the
Prisons*, 1784.

Jim's arrest for poaching was typical of the period, during
which gaming laws were tightened and an increasing number of
people were convicted for poaching (accounting for one in seven of
all criminal convictions by 1827). The law favoured the propertied
and was heavily weighted against the poor, as the contemporary
playwright Oliver Goldsmith wrote: 'Laws grind the poor, and
rich men rule the law'.

Rich men, as in the landed gentry, certainly administered
the law, and the protection of all property remained central
to eighteenth-century legislation. In Cornish society, although
smuggling was looked on with tolerance, the poacher (in the
words of Winston Graham) 'not only trespassed literally upon
someone's land, he trespassed metaphorically upon all the
inalienable rights of personal property. He was an outlaw and a
felon. Hanging was barely good enough.'

Punishments meted out were also severe. Prisoners on trial
were not allowed to give evidence, other than to answer 'guilty'
or 'not guilty' (and those who refused to answer were stretched
out on the ground and pressed with heavy weights until they did
speak). The courts, presided over by magistrates and justices of
the peace, or JPs (who were required to have an estate of £100
a year), dealt with crimes relating to property with exemplary
harshness, the list of crimes punishable by death – from petty
theft to sheep-stealing to poaching – increasing four-fold during
the eighteenth century.

ROSS (after Jim
has died)

*'The magistrates
should have been
there. Smug,
self-satisfied
upholders of the
law – and so
called gentlemen
who prize game
above honest
working men.
He tried to feed
his family. How
is that a crime?
By God, I could
commit murder
myself.'*

Public executions were hugely popular. Often the condemned man was paraded through the crowd on a cart, which also carried his coffin.

Whilst murderers could be given a nominal sentence, many of those guilty of theft were sentenced to hang (although thankfully the judicial process also facilitated the pardoning, lessening or redefinition of charges so that defendants could be spared the gallows). Those who did hang often did so in public, in front of a large crowd of jeering onlookers.

Crime *and* Punishment

Jim Carter escaped hanging but his sentence of two years in prison was in effect a death sentence. Prisons were notorious for their appalling conditions, and Jim, with a lung complaint (convulsive asthma as Dr Choake puts it), stood little chance of survival. Prisoners were thrown together, often in over-crowded dungeon-like conditions with little food or supervision, many waiting months or even years for trial or transportation. Under such dire conditions, prisoners simply rotted and outbreaks of

'gaol fever', which included typhus and smallpox, took a large death toll. Dr Johnson claimed that 'all the complicated horrors of a prison put an end every year to the life of one in four of those that are shut up from the common comforts of human life.'

Other forms of punishment included transportation, criminals first being deported to the American colonies of Maryland and Virginia in 1718. The American War of Independence, however, ended this and criminals were instead held in prisons or prison ships (known as hulks). In response to worsening overcrowding amongst prison populations, offenders, many of them convicted of petty theft, were from 1786 transported to the new colony at Botany Bay in Australia. Punishments for lesser offences included branding, which lasted until nearly the end of the eighteenth century, whipping (the victim being tied to a cart and run through the streets), flogging (often in front of a crowd) and the pillory, although this wasn't as popular a punishment as in earlier centuries.

Jud said he knew a man who was sent to Bodmin Gaol for next to nothing, and the first day he was there he got the fever and the second day he was dead.

From the novel *Ross Poldark*

The workhouse was reserved for those who couldn't earn their keep, the old, the sick and women with children. It was seen as an efficient way for parishes to fulfil their duties of care. By 1776 there were over 1800 workhouses in England and Wales with a total capacity of more than 90,000.

A Different Breed

The dire economic circumstances of the 1780s, with the continuing rise in unemployment and food prices, led to a rocketing of crime and general lawlessness, as the desperate and the starving took to poaching, smuggling or petty theft to feed themselves or top up their meagre incomes. Taxes were raised to fund the government debt, with excises falling on the most basic commodities, and this naturally hit the poorest the hardest. Winston Graham summarized the economic climate in *Ross Poldark*: 'taxes had gone up 20 per cent in five years and the new ones were dangerously unpopular. Land tax, house tax, servants' tax, window tax. Horses and hats, bricks and tiles, linen and calicoes. Another impost on candles hit directly at the poor. Last winter the fishermen of Fowey had saved their families from starvation by feeding them on limpets.'

Relief for the poor revolved round the poor laws, administered by individual parishes and funded by poor rates. Those who possessed 'settlement' in a particular parish could receive some relief, such as money for rent, house repairs or clothes, although great droves of the sick and needy could be driven out of the parish if they were deemed outside its responsibility. Alongside free handouts, however, was the belief that the poor should earn their keep, preferably in one of the hundreds of workhouses set up in many parishes of England and Wales in the eighteenth century. In reality the workhouses housed only the very sick and infirm, the very young and the aged, their death rates shockingly high. The philanthropist Jonas Hanway wrote that an infant aged between one and three would survive an average of just one month in a London workhouse.

Any attempt to improve the lot of the poor, however, was obstructed by a widespread belief that the masses were 'feckless' and prone to idleness and drunkenness, with many believing that wages should be kept as low as possible in order to encourage industriousness amongst the lower classes. The divide between rich and poor led to mutual distrust and bigotry, with those higher up the social ladder regarding the great mass of working poor as almost a different species. Dr Choake's indifference to Jim Carter's fate illustrates this well: 'No good will come of being sentimental about such folk. They're a different breed, sir. And should be treated as such.'

For the most past they were weakly, stinking, rachitic, pockmarked, in rags — far less well found than the farm animals which were being bought and sold. Was it surprising that the upper classes looked on themselves as a race apart?

Ross watches the poor go past at Redruth Fair, in *Ross Poldark*

Jud is capable of work, but not inclined to do any. His parish would thus probably refuse him any assistance.

The scything scene, in which we see Ross, pent up and shirt-less, hacking away at long grass, caused a real stir amongst Poldark *fans. Many delighted in Aidan Turner's muscled torso, although some criticized his use of the scythe.*

In fact, the production team did bring in a scything expert but they felt that the small scything movements he demonstrated didn't match Ross's emotional turmoil. They had to consider the wider story arc of the drama: Ross has just slept with Demelza for the first time and is still furious about Jim's prison sentence; and Demelza is watching him, reliving all the events and emotions of the night before and probably wondering what will now happen to her relationship with this handsome gentleman employer, whom she holds on a pedestal. So the production team encouraged Aidan to handle the scythe with a little more vigour. A disappointment perhaps to scything experts but it added to the dramatic pace of the story and made for a memorable scene.

Chapter Four

Ross and Demelza's marriage shocks Trenwith and Charles Poldark is stricken with a heart attack. Verity teaches Demelza how to become a refined lady and they become firm friends. Ross and Demelza are invited to Trenwith for Christmas, where everyone is enchanted by Demelza's singing. Ross's investors begin to withdraw their support from Wheal Leisure, until the mine finally hits copper to everyone's great relief. There is further good news when Demelza tells Ross she is pregnant.

Jack Farthing *is* George Warleggan

From humble beginnings as blacksmiths, the Warleggans have strived to become one of the wealthiest and most powerful families in Cornwall. The youngest member of the family, George Warleggan, is an ambitious banker who will stop at nothing to make a profit, even it means seeing his closest friends financially ruined.

They alone stood for the new-rich of the county. The elder Warleggan's father had been a country blacksmith who had begun tin-smelting in a small way; the smelter's son, Nicholas, had moved to Truro and built up a smelting works. From these roots all the tentacles of their fortune had sprung.

From the novel *Ross Poldark*

A constant devil on George's shoulder is his uncle Cary Warleggan (played by Pip Torrens), who increasingly presses George to make callous business decisions. Cary himself maintains a coarse edge that betrays his working-class upbringing and can be an acute embarrassment to George.

Playing George Warleggan is English actor Jack Farthing, whose former roles include Freddie Threepwood in the BBC's *Blandings* as well as George Balfour in the film *The Riot Club*. When it came to George Warleggan, Jack particularly enjoyed getting to grips with the role, as he explains: 'George is a layered and elaborate character. Some people would call him a villain but I shy away from that description – what makes him so exciting is that he is like any one of us; full of jealousy and resentment, he motivates himself and has this vast ambition and inability to decide what he wants. It has been very satisfying to get my teeth into the character.'

When Ross returns to Cornwall, George seems to show mixed feelings towards him. George freely admits that when they were at school, he admired Ross because 'he said what he thought, did what he liked' which, as George puts it, got him a 'following'. Since then, years of simmering resentment have built up, although George still clearly yearns for the respect and popularity that Ross so easily attains.

GEORGE

'At school I rather admired him.
He said what he thought,
did what he liked.'

CARY (surprised)

'And where did that get him?'

GEORGE

'It got him a following.
Something we frequently
fail to acquire.'

'Ross has the ability to make George feel small,' says Jack. 'Ross doesn't give him the respect that George thinks he deserves. George is fighting against not having a family name, not being of aristocratic lineage, so all of his class and elegance is kind of painted on and he knows that. Ross more than anyone reminds him of that.'

Amid the financial crisis of the late eighteenth century, the Warleggan family are flourishing as bankers and industrialists, gaining such power that they have the ability to make or break businesses, putting a stranglehold on the mining industry across Cornwall. George is aware that they have success and money, but as Jack says, 'George wants more, he wants respect. He wants popularity and doesn't want to be seen as an upstart or looked down on. He wants subtler things than just money.'

Jack Farthing: 'I feel I missed out on a lot of Cornwall as many of my scenes were filmed in interiors. You don't catch George on a horse much, he's in beautiful carriages, in houses and Truro rather than roaming around the coastline like Ross.'

While Ross is away, George becomes friends with Francis, which is partly a political move on George's part although Francis also benefits from George's financial support. Francis, however, fares badly under the influence of George and his rather unsavoury social circle, as he descends into drinking, gaming and adultery.

George is far from a two-dimensional character and we see changes in him through the series, as Jack explains: 'At the beginning he is less sure of how to wants to live and do business. He's probably a bit vulnerable and still working things out for himself. Through the influence of his uncle, however, and by fighting against the way society perceives him and through a growing anger towards Ross and feeling diminished by him, George is driven to become something harder and fiercer in the business sense, and I guess in every sense.'

George increasingly targets Ross, forcing his investors into bankruptcy and doing everything he can to ruin his fledgling smelting business. 'George has got his own demons, which sometimes makes him behave in a way that's morally

GEORGE

'What is it that offends you, Ross? That we Warleggans have dared to drag ourselves out of poverty and aspire to gentility?'

ROSS

'Poverty doesn't offend me. Nor does aspiration. But you're mistaken if you think greed and exploitation are the marks of a gentleman.'

Right: *For Jack one of the most important elements to the character is his appearance. 'More than most George cares about the way he looks,' says Jack Farthing. 'He is on show and is a man of fashion and elegance and slightly ahead of his time.'*

'I feel like it's very difficult to work out exactly where you are with a character until you work out the costume. The costumes played a huge part, and really helped with creating the whole image. You need to be aware that George is putting on a costume and presenting himself to society.'

reprehensible,' says Jack, 'although he actually gets much more satisfaction from a fair victory than an underhand one, so there are times in the series he's ashamed of his underhand means, which I think is an important part of him.'

As the series progresses, we become aware of George's admiration for Elizabeth. When Francis gambles away much of his inheritance, George steps in and says he will cancel their debts – the unspoken reason being that he loves Elizabeth. 'There's nothing untoward in the way he behaves,' says Jack. 'And then he finally plucks up the courage to make his feelings clear to Elizabeth and that's where we leave them at the end of the first series.'

It was hardly credible that a single generation divided a tough, gnarled old man who sat in a cottage in his shirt sleeves and chewed tobacco and could barely write his name from this cultured young man in a new-fashioned tight-cut pink coat with buff lapels.

From the novel *Ross Poldark*

A New Aristocracy

The Warleggans – a name Winston Graham chose, incidentally, after a village on Bodmin Moor – had risen in just two generations from humble beginnings to one of the richest and most powerful families in the county. The elder Warleggan, we are told, was a blacksmith who had begun tin-smelting, his son Nicholas had set up a smelting works and from this they had built up a large fortune.

It marks a dramatic rise in fortune and social mobility, a rags-to-riches story that has parallels with the history of the period. With an expansion of industry and trade (export trade doubled between 1714 and 1760), and a growing population (from 5.5 million in 1700 to just over 9 million in 1801), the British economy was buzzing with activity. As Dr Hannah Greig, historical adviser to the *Poldark* series, says, 'There was a sense of a world of opportunity, the idea you can make it if you want to. There are lots of new commercial opportunities in the eighteenth century – in global trade, shipping, financial services and the growth in consumer goods. British society is transforming before people's eyes.'

Those who benefitted from this new climate included the printer John Baskerville (1706–75), who began his adult life as a footman, and Lancelot 'Capability' Brown (1716–83), chief gardener to the aristocracy, who was the son of a small tradesman.

Printer John Baskerville rose through the ranks of society and is best known for designing an elegant new style of typography. This book is set in a font bearing his name.

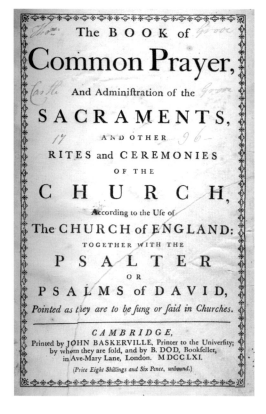

The BOOK of
Common Prayer,
And Adminiſtration of the
SACRAMENTS,
AND OTHER
RITES and CEREMONIES
OF THE
CHURCH,
According to the Uſe of
The CHURCH of ENGLAND:
TOGETHER WITH THE
PSALTER
OR
PSALMS of DAVID,
Pointed as they are to be ſung or ſaid in Churches.

CAMBRIDGE,
Printed by JOHN BASKERVILLE, Printer to the Univerſity; by whom they are ſold, and by B. DOD, Bookſeller, in Ave-Mary Lane, London. MDCCLXI.
(Price Eight Shillings and Six Pence, unbound.)

As Dr Johnson remarked: 'There was never from the earliest ages a time in which trade so much engaged the attention of mankind, or commercial gain was sought with such general emulation.'

Cornwall, with its booming mining industry, was certainly no exception and great fortunes could be made by enterprising individuals. William Lemon began life as the son of a poor man in Germoe. He found employment with the inventor of the horse-whim engine, John Coster, before rising to become manager of the Chyandour tin-smelting house at Penzance. He then invested in the aptly named Wheal Fortune (which earned him £10,000), worked the Gwennap mines, bought the great estate of Carclew and died a baronet in 1760.

These meteoric rises, however, were still fairly exceptional and the great majority of Cornish people profited little. And those that did acquire new wealth were, as George Warleggan feared, not always welcomed with open arms by the Establishment.

The behaviour of the aristocracy was a source of endless fascination . . . to themselves, at least.

FRONT, SIDE VIEW and BACK FRONT of a MALE and FEMALE CROP.

The social pecking order was still riven with tension, and some viewed this 'new aristocracy' as an unwelcome disruption to the status quo, in particular the unwritten rule that those at the top were responsible for the lower orders dependent upon them. The Poldarks, their pedigree stretching back generations, have always had, we are told, good relations with their tenants: the newly rich Warleggans, on the other hand, are ruthless and lacking any such social responsibilities.

Dr Hannah Greig agrees: 'Ross is fulfilling the role of an archetypal eighteenth-century gentleman, which some of the people around him are neglecting to do. That's why people were so suspicious of the local upstarts, as it was felt they weren't fulfilling their obligations. There was a belief that if you weren't born into landowning responsibilities then you might pursue your own self-interests over and above the needs of the community. That's one of the deeply ingrained ideas that operate in the hierarchy of the eighteenth-century world. It creates a lot of tension and *Poldark* explores that sense of change and pressure really well.'

Above: *Satirists delighted in poking fun at the styles of the newly wealthy; this dates from 1781.*
Right: *Though he may not always look it, Ross is most definitely a gentleman.*

The film crew prepare for a scene with Kyle Soller and Warren Clarke.

WARREN CLARKE *is* Charles Poldark

Sadly, Charles Poldark was Warren Clarke's final television role. A popular and versatile actor, known for numerous television and film roles, including *Dalziel and Pascoe* and Stanley Kubrick's *A Clockwork Orange*, Warren died suddenly at the age of sixty-seven just after he had finished filming *Poldark*. The cast and production team were shocked and deeply saddened by his death and dedicated the first episode of the series to him.

The role that Warren so expertly played was that of the imposing patriarch of Trenwith, whose presence fills every room. He longs for his son Francis to be more like his nephew Ross, but concedes that Francis lacks the gumption and aptitude to take over the family business.

After Charles learns of Ross's wedding, a heart attack confines him to his bed. In a moving final moment, the dying Charles grabs his nephew Ross's hand and declares: 'I've lost

Left: *The production designers added a portrait of Charles Poldark to the existing paintings at Trenwith.*
Right: *Robert Daws (Dr Choake): 'Warren had a good time on set and a great sense of humour. No one knew that Charles Poldark could do a Tommy Cooper impression.'*

all faith – in this world of ours – and my legacy. We both know Francis is not the man you are . . . Look after him for me . . . And our family . . . and our good name.'

Executive producer Karen Thrussell says: 'Warren was such a brilliant choice for the role, absolutely perfect, this larger-than-life character at the head of the Poldark clan, who's always very rude to Francis and knows that Ross is the better man,' and adds, 'Warren played Charles beautifully with humour and gravitas.'

Many in the cast and crew had worked with Warren before, including Robert Daws, who played Dr Choake: 'I was there on his last day of filming at St Just. He just got off his horse after the very last shot, said, "That's it, I'm done," cracked a joke, everyone on set fell about laughing and then off he went – and I don't think he was in front of a camera again. It was both sad and very special, and I'll miss him.'

Screenwriter Debbie Horsfield also commented: 'One of my long-term ambitions had been to work with Warren, a wonderful actor and also a fellow Mancunian. I feel immensely privileged that his final TV appearance was as the patriarch Charles Poldark – a character, who, like Warren, dominates the screen, makes you laugh out loud and breaks your heart.'

CHARLES
'Step up to the mark. You do recall that we have a mine?'

FRANCIS
'Yes, but . . .'

CHARLES
'It requires presence. Direction. Leadership. Yours. YOURS!'

Storm o' Pilchards

Frequently during the *Poldark* series we see villagers perched on the cliff tops looking out towards sea. They are on the lookout for pilchards, millions of which arrive in great shoals close to the shores of Cornwall in late summer. As the timing and location of their arrival vary – and in *Poldark* they arrive worryingly late – lookouts would be posted at good vantage points to make sure they weren't missed. Once a 'huer', as they were known, saw the familiar dark red tinge of a shoal of pilchards, he would call out, 'Heva! Heva!' and the locals would immediately down tools and help bring in the haul. Rowing boats would be launched and the huers would guide them out to the pilchards' location. Large seine nets would then surround and trap the shoal, before dragging them to shallower water where the fish could be transferred to a boat.

For a Cornish community, the pilchards were a very welcome and, indeed, vital catch, which enabled them to survive the winter when fresh food stocks were low. Once ashore, the

ROSS
'Good day, ladies. Are we expecting a storm?'

MRS ZACKY
'Storm o' pilchards, God willin'!'

ROSS
'They're late this year.'

MRS ZACKY
'An' we'll starve. Simple as that.'
(They both look worried. It's a very real possibility.)

ROSS
'Let's hope it won't come to that.'

Right: *The lookout point at Portreath, where the huer watched for fish.*

To salt a thousand fish, enough to support his family through the winter, a man had to buy seventy pounds of salt – which after tax increases could cost him more than a month's wages.

Organized fishing communities could make good money from exporting pilchards. Between 1747 and 1756 the ports of Fowey, Falmouth, Penzance and St Ives exported around 30,000 hogsheads (barrels) a year. Each hogshead contained up to 3,000 fish. But the trade was unreliable; in 1785 and 1786 fewer than 7,000 hogsheads were caught in the whole of Cornwall.

Exports of salted pilchards peaked in 1871 but from the 1880s the industry began to go into terminal decline partly as a result of a drop in demand from overseas markets.

pilchards were gutted and stacked in layers of salt, where they could be stored for weeks or even sold and exported over large distances. Many fishing villages also had cellars where the pilchards could be placed in stone tanks, salted and pressed, with the oil that was drained off used for lighting. The lamps that burnt pilchard oil, known as chill lamps, would give off a strong, fishy smell. In the *Poldark* novels Mrs Zacky makes her family drink the oil to keep them strong and healthy.

Ross
*'I hope you won't live to regret
your choice of a husband.'*

Demelza
'Why would I?'

Ross
'We may soon be destitute.'

Demelza
'There's other kind of treasure.'

Drunk *for a* Penny

Drinking was a popular pastime in the eighteenth century, as it is in the world of the Poldarks. All classes liked an alcoholic tipple, from the likes of Jud and Prudie to Francis Poldark, as a means of idle merriment or a pathway to oblivion. Drunkenness was seen by many as a vice much loved by the Englishman (and woman), the Swiss traveller Cesar de Saussure (1705–83) remarking: 'It is not the lower populace alone that is addicted to drunkenness; numbers of persons of high rank and even of distinction are over fond of liquor.'

England was awash with inns, taverns and ale-houses – with a population of just 5,000, Northampton in this period had some sixty inns and a hundred ale-houses. As with the fictional Red Lion in Truro, inns and similar drinking establishments served a variety of purposes, from venues for business meetings and auctions to lodgings for travellers and local prostitutes.

Spirits such as brandy, rum, whisky and gin were comparatively cheap and easily available, largely as a result of the large quantities smuggled in, a practice especially common in Cornwall. When the government placed a heavy tax on French brandy, it merely fuelled the gin craze of the first half of the eighteenth century. Cheaper than beer, gin consumption, especially amongst the poor, increased rapidly, with gin shops advertising 'Drunk for a penny, dead drunk for tuppence, straw free'. By 1742 it's estimated that the population of England, which was a tenth of today's, drank 19 million gallons of gin, ten times more than today.

William Beckford, *A History of Cornwall*, 1787

A visit to the Consolidated Mines of Gwennap

Several woeful figures in tattered garments with pickaxes on their shoulders crawled out of a dark fissure and repaired to a hovel, which I learnt was a gin-shop. There they pass the few hours allotted them aboveground and drink, it is to be hoped, in oblivion of their subterranean existence. Piety, as well as gin, helps to fill up their leisure moments, and I was told that Wesley, who came apostolising into Cornwall a few years ago, preached on this very spot to about 7,000 followers. Since the period Methodism has made a very rapid progress and has been of not trifling service in diverting the attention of these sons of darkness from their present condition to the glories of the life to come.

Left and right:

Hogarth's famous pair of prints from 1751, Beer Street *and* Gin Lane. *Imported gin was blamed for many of society's ills, especially when compared to good honest British beer. The popularity of gin caused other problems: it drove up the price of grain, making bread more expensive.*

CHAPTER FIVE

Ross and Demelza welcome two new arrivals: Dwight Enys, a doctor who plans to make a study of miners' lung diseases, and their own baby daughter, Julia Grace Poldark. Villager and miner Mark falls in love with and marries the capricious Keren, a member of a travelling acting group. With other mine owners, Ross sets about building his own smelting company. In a bid to reconcile with Captain Blamey, Demelza leads Verity to town, where there is a riot over the price of corn. Francis, unhappy with his marriage to Elizabeth, spends what little money he has on Margaret, an ambitious prostitute, and finally gambles the family mine on a game of cards.

The arrival of the young, dedicated doctor Dwight Enys is a welcome relief to those working the mines of the Poldark estate. Until then, the only medic for miles around was the snobbish Dr Choake, who treats only those who can afford his fees.

Casting aspersions on Enys's more modern techniques, Choake is a firm advocate of leeches and bleeding, inflicting his outmoded and potentially lethal methods on his unfortunate patients. He also becomes an ever-grumbling stakeholder in Wheal Leisure, although his increasing disapproval of Ross's disregard for his class leads him eventually to sell his shares to George Warleggan.

LUKE NORRIS *is* Dwight Enys

Ross is delighted to see his old friend Dwight Enys again and warmly welcomes him to Cornwall. As comrade soldiers fighting in America, we learn that Dwight, as a young army surgeon, attended to Ross's injuries. He also shared with Ross some sympathy for the revolutionary aims of the American people: namely liberty and democracy.

This egalitarian spirit runs through much of his work, his visit to Nampara enabling him to study the diseases that afflict miners. Unlike Dr Choake, who is mainly interested in treating the great and the good of the county, Dwight attends to the poor and whoever is in need, and is tireless in his work. He no doubt would have approved of the principles of the NHS, the free and comprehensive healthcare service being set up in Britain just at the time that Winston Graham was writing the early *Poldark* novels.

DOCTOR ENYS
'I came here to heal my patients, not bankrupt them.'

Graham's son Andrew adds, 'Enys wants to treat people who he thinks he can really help (and not just who can pay his fees like Choake). It's the late eighteenth century, and medicine is beginning to move away from the old-fashioned methods. Enys tries something and if that doesn't work he just tries something else. He's in very sharp contrast to Dr Choake and others like him who just bleed away as if that's the only thing to do.'

Playing the handsome Dr Enys is Luke Norris, an established theatre actor who has also written for the stage and screen. *Poldark* is his biggest television role to date although he has made numerous appearances in film and television, including *The Duchess*, *The Inbetweeners* and *Skins*.

As the series progresses, we see Dwight at first resist and then succumb to the flirtations of Mark's pretty wife, Keren – an infidelity that has tragic consequences for her. Dwight, at great risk, helps Ross rescue Jim Carter from prison, and cares determinedly for Demelza and Julia when they are struck ill. As Luke Norris says, 'Dwight really is a nice guy but I guess the challenge is not to make him too much of a goody-goody. Like many of the *Poldark* characters, he has his flaws – but essentially he has a good heart.'

Luke Norris: 'I hadn't ridden a horse since I was eight and I was thrown in the deep end a bit when I arrived in Cornwall for filming. My first scene was Dwight arriving on horseback coming down a cliff!'

The Carnmore Copper Company

In a bid to break the Warleggans' stranglehold on the copper prices in Cornwall, Ross, with other investors, secretly attempts to start his own smelting company, the Carnmore Copper Company.

Here again Winston Graham based this on a similar attempt by the real-life Cornish Metal Company (CMCo), which was established in 1784 to compete against the companies of South Wales and Bristol. Between 1784 and 1792, the CMCo attempted to rescue the industry by buying all copper ore raised, having it converted to copper and attempting to market it, but with little success. Ross Poldark's Carnmore Copper Company is dissolved after only a year, as other smelting companies, backed by the Warleggans, price them out of the market and starve them of the copper ore they need to survive.

Smelting is the process of taking copper ore and passing it through a series of furnaces in order to separate it from impurities such as sulphur. The smelting companies bought the ore at auction by means of a 'ticketing' system. Agents would inspect 'doles' of copper at the mines and would then meet at an inn where they would hand in sealed bids or tickets. The chairman would open the bids and the highest bidder won.

During the eighteenth century, it was rumoured that the smelting companies colluded to keep the copper prices artificially low (as the Warleggans do) to maximize their profits. The practice caused widespread resentment, particularly amongst mining workers who were similarly affected by low copper prices. As Jack Tripp complains in the first *Poldark* novel: 'Why is there no work in the mines? Because the tin and copper prices are so low. But why are they so low, friends? Because the merchants and the smelters fix the prices among themselves to suit themselves.'

Ross

*'You were right.
The world is a harder
place now.
Thanks to Julia.*

*Stakes are higher.
Losses more painful.'*

ROBERT DAWS *is* Dr Choake

Playing Dr Choake is Robert Daws, an accomplished actor with an extensive acting career in theatre and television, including *The Royal* and *Outside Edge*. Robert thoroughly enjoyed working on *Poldark*, principally because the scripts and characters were so well written. 'Choake is a ghastly old curmudgeon – he's a man without any real social conscience, but, like so many of those of those who populate the *Poldark* world, he's a really vivid character and it was great fun to play him.'

Choake's victims include the ailing Charles Poldark, who only rallies, Francis claims, 'Despite Choake's efforts!' He also oversees Elizabeth's labour, claiming afterwards, in a typically odious manner, that women 'make a song and dance about it'.

Robert was fascinated by Dr Choake's antiquated methods of medicine, and admits he was inundated on social media and in the street by young people in particular keen to know more about the old techniques of bleeding and boiling. As Robert says, 'By the time Enys turns up you thank God that old git is on his way out, as Choake will leech you, bleed you and boil you to death.'

Hair maketh the man

When it came to getting into the character of Choake, Robert jokes that a certain element of his costume was crucial: 'I grew very attached to my little grey wig. I went to the fitting and it came out of the box and the make-up designer and I knew instinctively that this was Choake. I was relieved because it helped with the acting, I just needed the wig to turn up on set. As soon as the wig went on I was looking at Choake. If the wig could speak it would have saved a lot of money.'

Bleed, Blister *and* Purge

This was an era in which there were few advances in medicine, and many doctors were simply groping in the dark when it came to the treatment of most diseases. Some, like Dr Choake, clung to methods that had been used for millennia whilst other types of 'quack' doctors or 'mountebanks' advocated a whole host of bizarre and ineffective remedies, from 'nervous cordials' to 'electricity treatment' and 'bathing in earth'.

The eighteenth-century physician usually graduated from a university, although medical degrees from Oxford and Cambridge could often be bought. A physician was in effect a general practitioner to anyone who could afford his fees, and those that couldn't probably had a lucky escape when it came to Dr Choake. Unaware of the hazards of germs, doctors rarely washed their hands, which in turn led to the spread of infection, particularly during childbirth.

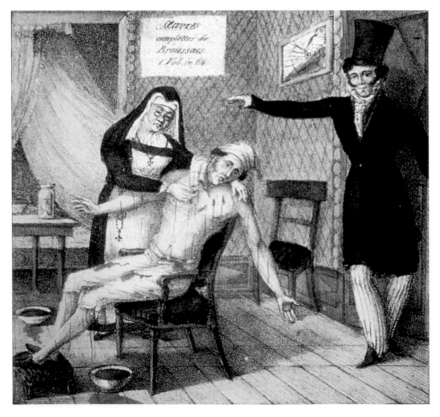

Dr Broussais looks on while a nun uses leeches to bleed his patient. Francois Broussais (1772–1838) was a French physician whose advocacy of bleeding, leech treatments, and fasting dominated Parisian medical practice in the early nineteenth century.

Stopping at nothing to inflict his outmoded treatments on patients, Dr Choake is a great fan of blood-letting, which involves withdrawing blood from a patient, sometimes with the use of leeches. A treatment that dates back to antiquity, the practice is generally entirely ineffective against disease and, if anything, harmful as it weakens patients, making them more susceptible to infection. By the end of the eighteenth century the benefits of bloodletting had begun to be seriously questioned although many doctors, like Dr Choake, were still firm advocates.

Thomas Rowlandson drew three series of comic scenes involving Doctor Syntax on his travels around Britain. Here the Doctor is being cupped to treat his bruises: a cut is made in the bruise and a hot cup placed over it. As the air cools and contracts in the cup, it sucks blood from the bruise.

Other treatments mentioned by Choake include blistering (i.e., anything used to induce a blister), which was a popular treatment for insanity in the eighteenth century, and forced vomiting and enemas, which were alternative ways to purge ailments out of patients' bodies. Choake's patients grow ever more weary of his methods – Verity in the first *Poldark* novel describes his various treatments: 'One month he bleeds me and the next he tells me I am suffering from anaemia. Then he gives me potions that make me sick and vomits that don't. I doubt if he knows as much as the old women at the fair.'

Methodism

During Julia Grace's christening, Demelza's father, Tom Carne (played by Mark Frost), makes a surprise visit with his new wife, Nelly. Once a drunken brute of a man, who beat Demelza as a child, he has clearly gone through some kind of religious conversion, and is now determined to pass scorn on his new in-laws. On entering Nampara and seeing guests in fine clothes drinking port and rum, he utters, 'Step no further, Nelly. This be a place of filth and abomination.' Ruth Treneglos's low-cut dress causes further offence.

The new religion that Tom has succumbed to with such fervour is Methodism, an evangelical Protestant movement that swept through Britain in the eighteenth century. The people of Cornwall were particularly drawn to Methodism, its practice of preaching outdoors in barns and cottages suiting Cornwall's

TOM CARNE
'Cover yerself, missy. Your place is to be decent an' modest – not layin' out wares for men to slaver over.'

Gwennap Pit, near Redruth, where John Wesley preached to huge crowds. He travelled constantly, preaching two or three times a day.

rural population, many of whose villages were far from a parish church. Its founder John Wesley preached himself in the county many times, first visiting in 1743 and visiting another thirty-two times before his death in 1791.

With its simple doctrine of justification through faith and instant salvation, Methodism appealed to the poor, its preachers taking its message to labourers and criminals and those often excluded from organized religion. For the mining communities and fishermen of Cornwall, Methodism offered comfort and hope for those who confronted danger, uncertainty and hardship in their everyday lives. Preachers advocated abstinence from most forms of amusement and luxury, and in Cornwall huge crowds of up to 20,000 people were drawn to open-air meetings, such as at the abandoned mine of Gwennap Pit.

Rioting Mob

Discontent amongst the poor and hungry soon bubbles into rioting and violence, as witnessed by Verity, Demelza and Captain Blamey during a visit to Truro. The riot has erupted over the price of corn, a frequent occurrence in eighteenth-century Cornwall, when any increase in food prices could worsen the already-bleak conditions for the poor.

In the early eighteenth century it was normal for grain to be sold directly by the farmer at market; people bought what they needed – or received it as part of their wages – and had it ground by the miller, before making their own bread. By the time Ross Poldark returned from America, in most places millers or dealers bought all the grain direct from the farmers before the poor could buy any.

Anger at high prices was usually directed at the middlemen, the grain dealers and millers. The resentment came not only from the poor, but also from landowners who felt they were being exploited by upstart merchants making inflated profits after buying their grain. During years of bad harvest, discontent was also directed against those merchants who were known to export corn abroad, which was seen as unpatriotic.

As a result, food riots were common across England. In 1766–77, 3,000 troops were sent to quell food riots in Wiltshire and Somerset, which involved looting and attacks on shops. The City of London was paralysed in 1780 by the Gordon Riots. Fear of popery sparked the violence but rioters soon turned their

Gordon rioters are pressed back in the London streets by soldiers in June 1780.

A Legal Method of Thrashing out Grain or Forestallers & Regraters Reaping the Fruits of their Harvest

Ancient laws against forestallers (those who buy up a commodity before it reaches open market) and regraters (those who amass large quantities of a product to create a monopoly) were repealed in 1772. By 1800 this was widely seen as grossly unfair, as this cartoon shows.

On several occasions, rioters forcibly took over mills or stores of grain, and took the stock to market themselves. There it was sold at what they felt was a fair price, and the proceeds returned to the miller or farmer.

focus on the rich, looting and smashing breweries and Newgate Gaol until troops restored order. (Damage to property amounted to £100,000 – ten times as much as that inflicted on Paris throughout the French Revolution.)

In Cornwall, food riots in 1727 were followed two years later by an uprising of tinners, who 'ravaged up and down the country in a very insolent manner and great numbers'. Four of their leaders were hanged, but from that time on, there were riots in Cornwall at least once every decade, which caused real concern and fear amongst the gentry. The innovations brought by the Industrial Revolution also led to frequent strikes and outbursts of violence: in 1787, a serious riot by unemployed and starving miners broke out at Poldice Mine, with the adventurers blaming the miners' misery on the hefty premiums they had been forced to pay for the new steam engines manufactured by James Watt and his partner Matthew Boulton.

A Cornish 'Troyl'

The wedding of Mark and Keren is celebrated in true Cornish style with lots of dancing, music and merriment. Cornwall (then and now) has its own traditions of folklore, festival and legend, and music and dance are a central part of its culture. To recreate the wedding scene with some authenticity, the production team brought in the services of Merv Davey, the 'Grand Bard of Cornwall' and an expert in folk tradition and dance.

The dance we see is typically Cornish and known as the Serpent Dance. Like many of Cornwall's dances, its origins are medieval, when it was known as a 'farandole'. Cornwall had preserved many of its medieval cultural traditions, which elsewhere had been swept away by the Protestant Reformation. Methodism, which was very popular in Cornwall at the time, embraced folk dancing and this served to preserve the art, keeping it very much alive in the *Poldark* era.

The wedding of Jim and Jinny also shows a traditional barn dance (or 'troyl' as it is known in Cornish dialect), the Newlyn Reel, with Merv Davey playing the Cornish bagpipes alongside the drums and fiddle. Merv's wife Alison was also on hand to help with teaching the cast to dance, whilst daughter Jowdy and son Cas were amongst the dancers, alongside a few other representatives from traditional Cornish dance groups.

POLDARK
ROLL
#B 96
SLATE
X31
TAKE
2
MOS
SCENE
SC.2/42
DIR: ED BAZALGETTE
DOP: CINDERS FORSHAW
B
DATE: 9.6.2014 [redacted]S/SYNC

Interview with CATRIN MEREDYDD, Production Designer

How do you describe your job?

As a production designer, your main job is to create a convincing world from the script. Our department is responsible for all the sets, the interiors and the builds; we also build on location. We deal with special effects, we deal with the animals, the horses and carriages, we do graphics . . . Basically we do everything other than what they wear! If there's a handbag, it might be us or it might be costume design, but if they take something out of it, that's from production design.

There's an incredibly diverse group of people in our department, because you've got graphic designers, set decorators, prop men, carpenters, painters, model-makers, animal-handlers . . . it's such a fantastic mix of people. The art department requires a lot of team work, and we had a fabulous team.

How did you find the locations?
As a production designer you go with the director to source locations. Local location scouts offer you places, and we looked ourselves as well. We went down to Cornwall quite early on, with Ed [Bazalgette, director] and Eliza [Mellor, producer] and Carn [Burton, location manager] and we went down mines, climbed down cliffs . . .

Did you do any filming in a real mine?
We did very little in an actual mine, because the practicalities of it are quite restricted. We did a couple of small scenes in Poldark Mine, just one day's shoot, because we needed to flood the mine, and we needed close-ups of cutting into real rock. So it helped us to be in the real space. But the majority of it happened on set. There was a stunt scene, with an actor half-drowning, so for safety reasons we needed that to be in a controlled environment. But it was crucial to go to the real mines, to Poldark and Geevor. A fantastic mines

Above: *The Wheal Leisure mine was constructed in the Bottle Yard studios in Bristol.* **Left:** *Catrin at Ross's desk in Nampara.*

advisor from Levant gave us a lot of historical references and research. Many people kindly gave us a lot of help, so we could get all the detail correct.

For the exteriors of the mine we clad onto an existing mine engine house at Wheal Owles (see page 46). We had to show the progression of the mine from when Ross first inherited it, almost derelict, to it being a busy going concern at the end of the series. The idea was, in this series, that the beam engine isn't working again yet, but they always had a backup horse-driven pump to empty water out of the mine. They were basically working under sea level; the chances of flooding were quite high. It was incredibly dangerous.

Nampara was an important location and set. The first drawing we did was Nampara. We went down to Cornwall and looked at quite a lot of houses, including the original house that was used [for the first *Poldark* series] but it's the nature of the time we live in, a lot of Cornwall now has been gentrified, and there's a lot of things we shouldn't see. There are a lot of palm trees now, which wouldn't have been there then. And so we eventually ended up on Bodmin Moor, at a beautiful house that had retained a lot of its original features. It also gave us an almost 360-degree view around it, and a back yard, which we were able to use a lot. And then from that, I could begin to design the interior of Nampara, but make it slightly bigger, with more windows to let in more light, and bigger rooms for action, and also a much, much bigger kitchen for all the things that go on there.

I'm a real stickler for continuity on thresholds. You always want it to be convincing when Ross walks out of the front door

Top: *The exterior of Nampara from a distance.*
Above: *Construction of the Nampara set in Bristol.*
Opposite: *The interior sets (left) for the parlour and kitchen; the exterior location before (top right) and after (bottom right) being dressed for filming.*

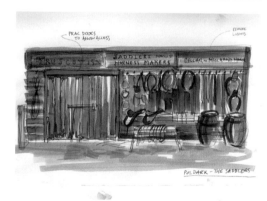

POLDARK : THE RED LION.

POLDARK - THE SADDLERS.

POLDARK - SILVERSMITH

Above: *Corsham in Wiltshire stood in for Truro.*
Opposite: *The post office became the haberdasher's. Other shops and houses became the saddler's and printseller's.*

of his house on set, into the yard on location. The join is very important, and I think we got away with it. It makes a set far more convincing to the audience. You can cheat size to a certain degree, but you always need to feel you're really in that house. It was important to feel that set was there on Bodmin Moor.

You sketched a lot of shop fronts for locations.
I much prefer it. A lot of people use Photoshop for concept art, but it's such a quick thing to be able to pick up a pencil and sketch what's in your head. You wouldn't believe the number of things that were done initially on a Post-it note or a scrap of paper, and then recalculated into something far more technical. I drew all the shop fronts we needed in Corsham in pen and ink. You can hand a drawing over to someone and instantly they know how it's dressed, what the colours are, get a sense of the business of the street.

Why did you use Corsham for Truro?

Because it's a conservation area, they haven't been allowed to change a lot of things. Essentially the foundation of the place lent itself quite well to the locations we needed – the pub, the haberdasher's, a good central area for a market. It has a steeple very similar to Truro's in the background. I found paintings of Truro in the 1780s, and they compared very well to Corsham now. Truro doesn't look anything like that now! We tried to find a location in Cornwall, but shooting in the summer, in the middle of a town . . . impossible. But Corsham allowed us to close the roads, and all the people were wonderful, they allowed us to dress the fronts of their shops and houses.

The streets of Corsham provided various locations for Truro, from the Red Lion pub to the market.

There was a large tent by the Red Lion with the pub name on it . . .
That was covering lampposts! We have to cover anything up to the head height of a man on horseback. Anything above that is taken out in post-production, and they did a really good job. They added a lot of ships' masts in the background.

For the Red Lion, we had the exterior on location in Corsham, and a little 'airlock' behind the door on location that matched the set in the studio. I really liked the Red Lion; I think every series needs a pub. It's where lots of things can happen, people can bump into each other. It's a good story area, you can move a story on in a pub. Also it's where they did all the meetings; pubs were the local banks, where you did business. The logos of banks are often similar to old pub signs.

How does Trenwith compare to the Warleggan house?
Trenwith was a location near Bristol called
Chavenage House. We looked at quite a few
country houses. It needed to be a much older style
of architecture, with oriel windows and heavy
Tudor panelling, to give you the weight of the
family, that they were an old established family. We
needed a house that reflected that. And it was great
to have the grand hall and then the small oak room
off it; you could always have small scenes there with
the bigger scene happening in the background.
So the geography of the place worked really well
for us. We had the bedrooms there, too. Most of
Trenwith was on location. And Ross and Demelza
got married in Chavenage Chapel.

We wanted a real lift for the Warleggans, we
wanted them to be the height of Georgian fashion.
Really colourful, with chandeliers, completely
modern . . . he would have had that built, so it
was new. It was filmed in and around Bristol in
several locations depending on what we needed – a
staircase, an entrance hall. They had artwork on
the walls that was of the period, but we brought in
all the furniture. You can't have a crowd scene with
the owner's furniture, in case it gets damaged. You can't really
replace that valuable stuff!

And you went to St Fagans National History Museum near Cardiff?
That was partly my doing, being Welsh! We did Captain
Blamey's house there. It wasn't featured much, so it didn't justify
a build. St Fagans gave us a few different interiors that we could
shoot all in two days, with a variety of style and texture, all in
one location. So we had the Captain's house, and the interior
of Doctor Enys's house. The exterior of that was not far from
Nampara on Bodmin Moor.

How do you get the props historically accurate?

I think the research done with the graphics, particularly, was very impressive. We went to the British Museum and used our historical contacts to make sure we were correct. We went down to Truro Museum, which had some great examples of things like copper specimens but also everyday items like banknotes. Helston Museum was also incredibly helpful. The local museums have more in-depth local knowledge and more mundane things like rum bottles, coins, baskets, casks, miners' hats with candles on . . . In the books, Winston Graham was incredibly good at research, so we had to try and do as well as we could.

Top: *The cross-section map of Wheal Leisure that Ross examines at his desk.*

I loved the fans we designed for the ball, which were historically accurate. They had the steps of the dance drawn on them. You'd find out in advance what dances were going to be played, and the correct moves were put on the fans. So while the ladies were fanning themselves, they could revise their footwork. Very clever!

Above: *The desk of Ross's banker, Harris Pascoe, needed a wide variety of documents.*
Right: *Demelza proves to be a much better cook than Prudie. The Cornish were famous – if not notorious – for making pies with contents barely considered food by the rest of the country. There used to be a proverb that the devil wouldn't set foot in Cornwall for fear of being put in a pie.*
Below: *The notebook in which Captain Blamey draws and names the sails of a ship for Verity.*

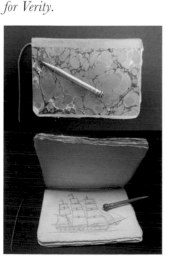

Do you think all your hard work was visible on screen?
You always put as much detail as possible into a scene, but inevitably some scenes are shot so quickly that some of the detail is missed. You can't *not* put it in, though, in case they decide on the day to go close in on something. Often the detail is where the story is. Props can tell a story very quickly – the food, for instance. Catherine Tidy made some amazing food. We sourced lots of research, and she had so much of her own knowledge. People really enjoy that level of detail in a period drama, it helps to immerse yourself in that way of life.

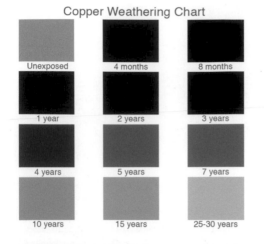

Copper Weathering Chart

Unexposed	4 months	8 months
1 year	2 years	3 years
4 years	5 years	7 years
10 years	15 years	25-30 years

How did you choose the colours for Poldark*?*

I wanted the colour palette of *Poldark* to look like Cornwall.
The landscapes sing out, they are so beautiful that you want
your designs to blend, you don't want anything to jump out too
much. We had to be sensitive to the landscape. I worked quite
closely with the costume designer early on with this one, putting
together mood boards based on copper. Copper starts as a rich
orange, reflected in Demelza's hair, but as it ages and oxidizes it

turns brown and then turquoise, the colour of the dress that she wears. I was using all those colours and so was Marianne the costume designer.

You were lucky with the weather.
We had one amazing day, when we did the fishing scene. We'd booked the lugger with traditional sails, and the pilchard baskets. We couldn't have wished for better. The scene is

Filming at Porthgwarra Beach.

very celebratory and happy, and so was the filming. Lots of ice creams were eaten by the crew, and lots of pilchards eaten by the seagulls. They were fed for months.

Filming at Charlestown harbour in Cornwall. Catrin: 'We dressed the harbour at Charlestown. It's such a great location for filming, with a sense of scale and the sea behind. We did the marriage of Blamey and Verity on a boat there.'

Who was responsible for all the flowers?
That was one of the things that came
from the books; Demelza is always
picking wild flowers. When we first
see Nampara it's in such a state of
disrepair, with dead chickens, and
rats running around. When Demelza
arrives she brings light and life. We
lightened the walls, cleaned the
windows and added lots of flowers.
Shonagh [Smith] our set decorator
and Cat McKail our standby art
director, they loved doing the flowers.

Are you pleased with your work on
Poldark?
I really enjoyed designing the series.
It's such a lovely period to do. All
the detail, the way of life . . . Just the
research was fascinating and I loved
bringing that to the screen. I think it's
a visually rich series, if you can see
past Aidan's pecs to the background!

One of the best compliments I had
was that it was seamless. We wanted
Poldark to have a sense of a beautiful
world that we could tell a love story
in, without anything jumping out or
distracting from that. Every part of the
design works together, is consistent
and harmonious.

I'm sure the world of *Poldark* will
continue to grow over the next series.
Maybe that beam engine at the mine
will finally work!

CHAPTER SIX

*The Carnmore Copper Company is a success, Ross making more
of an enemy of George Warleggan by outbidding him for copper at
auction. Discovering there is fever at Bodmin Gaol, Ross and Dwight
Enys force their way in and discover Jim near death; despite their best
efforts to save him, he dies. Ross attends George's grand ball although
he is sickened to be amongst the people who are responsible for Jim's
death. Ross, drinking heavily, leaves Demelza to fend for herself,
although she is clearly the belle of the ball. In a card game with
Matthew Sanson, Ross seems to wager recklessly, even staking Wheal
Leisure. Finally, Ross exposes Sanson as a cheat and humiliates him
in front of everyone. Ross is unaware that Sanson is a cousin of the
Warleggans, and that George will want revenge.*

PHIL DAVIS *is* Jud Paynter *and* BEATIE EDNEY *is* Prudie Paynter

Two characters that seem part of the very furniture of Ross's
ancestral home are Jud and Prudie. As former servants and
companions of his father, Ross is compelled to keep them on
despite all their obvious shortcomings. Lazy, frequently drunk,
and not averse to stealing from their master's drinks cabinet,
they amount to a wretched pair, but nonetheless provide much
entertainment during the series.

Playing Jud is Phil Davis, who has appeared in a host of
television and film roles, from *The Bounty* and *Vera Drake* to
Sherlock. Aware of the success of the previous adaptation,

Phil came to the *Poldark* series completely afresh but on reading Debbie Horsfield's scripts, he quickly warmed to the subject matter.

'The scripts give quite a gritty depiction of eighteenth-century life in Cornwall, with the mines closing and terrible poverty. For us now it's a shock to see just how difficult life was for the vast majority of people, particularly in places like Cornwall.'

Jud's sidekick, Prudie, is played by Beatie Edney, whose many television and film appearances include *Highlander*, *In the Name of the Father* and *Agatha Christie's Poirot*. Beatie was similarly taken with the subject matter of *Poldark*.

'I read the novels when we had started filming in Cornwall. They are very interesting about the social times, the tin mines and miners. But what's really striking is that nothing has really changed. Poor people are still poor and rich people still rich – people have to struggle. There was a recession in the tin-mining community and we've been going through a recession. Things haven't really changed.'

Beatie was also familiar with the history of the era, having starred as Queen Charlotte in a 2012 theatre production of *The Madness of King George*. 'But in that I was playing a queen and in this I'm playing a peasant with bad teeth,' says Beatie, 'although Queen Charlotte did have bad teeth too because she took snuff.'

When Ross returns to Nampara, he discovers that Jud and Prudie have moved in and have pretty much destroyed the house in the process, with chickens and goats in the sitting room. 'They've been left the responsibility of the estate and they're just not up to it at all,' explains Prudie. 'They're floundering – so it's not really their fault that they have goats in the sitting room. They don't really know any better. I saw it as if they were children, very naughty children.'

As servants to Ross, they continue to fall well below the mark, doing as little as possible around the house and constantly bickering. 'They're an incorrigible pair of rogues,' says Phil, 'and Jud is usually drunk on Ross's smuggled brandy and he gets into a lot of trouble.'

When Ross brings Demelza back to the house, the pair take an immediate dislike to her. 'Prudie totally disapproves of Demelza when she's first taken on,' says Beatie, 'until she discovers that Demelza will actually do all the work, so she's thrilled about that. She has a grudging respect for Ross, but she's not above stealing his booze. That changes as she starts to respect Demelza and she tells Jud off for stealing his master's drink. And by the end of the series she has a real respect for Ross.'

As the series progresses Prudie does improve and she and Demelza develop a friendship. Jud, however, shows no sign of improvement, largely because of his fondness for Ross's brandy. 'The secret to Jud is he's always slightly drunk – he's

Beatie Edney: 'I have to look of the period so they dirty me down a lot and I have scars and I'm not allowed to wear anything blue because apparently it makes my eyes look nice and I'm not allowed to look nice.'

never entirely sober,' says Phil. 'Even when he's quiet and contemplative, he will have had a drink. I'm often staggering around drunk or making some kind of pithy remark at the end of the scene.'

Together, the couple have a stormy love/hate relationship, which often descends into violence when they've had a drink. Prudie, however, gives as good as she gets and she is often seen clouting Jud. In one particular scene, they end up in a full-on brawl, which was carefully choreographed by a fight director.

'You never improvise this kind of thing,' says Beatie, 'it's always choreographed. If you're doing several takes you don't want to hit somebody five times because you're going to start hurting them.' Phil adds: 'We decided the safest thing to do was for Beatie to sit on me and for me to turn her over so I was sitting on her. And I'm just about to deliver the big blow before Demelza pulls me off.'

JUD

'Tedn' right – tedn' fair – tedn' just – tedn' fittin' –'

PRUDIE

'Hould yer clack, y'black worm, or I'll crown 'ee meself!'

They also had to get to grips with the Cornish accent, as Phil explains: 'We had some help from a dialect coach, which is very useful. She gave us some CDs to listen to and we muddled through. You've also got to be careful as it's important you are understood. And there is no one indigenous, correct Cornish accent because it's got all manner of influences and flavour from all over. When I had time off I would often go and play golf and sit in the golf club and listen to the accents around me.'

Eventually, in a drunken stupor, Jud takes things too far and insults Ross in front of Demelza, unaware that his master can hear every word. In a rage, Ross finally gives him his marching orders and Jud, accompanied by Prudie, leaves Nampara. They end up living in the hedgerows and finally in a barn on Ross's estate but continue to try and make Ross and Demelza guilty by walking forlornly past every time they see them.

When asked whether Jud will learn his lesson and improve his life, Phil thinks it very unlikely: 'Jud is incorrigible with very few redeeming features, which makes him such fun to play.'

Of the couple's role in the series, Phil adds: 'Jud and Prudie are comic relief and they are quite funny because they are so incredibly selfish. But they're not particularly lovable. They're thieves and drunks, and Jud is a violent man so there's an edge to it. But they stick together – partly because I don't suppose anyone else will put up with them.'

When asked about the public's reaction to the series, actors often say it's difficult to tell when filming, but Phil and Beatie's instincts were that that it would go down well with television audiences. 'People will love *Poldark* because it's got everything,' says Beatie. 'It's got a love story, wars, social realism, comedy, drama, costumes, beauty (I mean you only have to look at Aidan Turner, who's devastatingly good looking, and the girls are beautiful).' Phil is similarly upbeat about it: 'It's a swashbuckling, romantic adventure with a bit of political edge. It gives also an honest account of life in eighteenth-century Cornwall, and has a fantastic hero at the centre of it.'

CAROLINE BLAKISTON *is* Aunt Agatha

The formidable and aged matriarch Aunt Agatha is a forbidding presence at Trenwith. In her early nineties and decrepit, she provides a constant reminder of the ancient lineage of the Poldarks: 'Six generations of Poldarks I've seen,' she says on her first meeting with Demelza, 'Now what do'you think of that?'

In appearance Aunt Agatha is frail and thin although she has a surprisingly healthy appetite and is seemingly immune to illness, or at least the putrid throat that strikes down everyone else at Trenwith. Deaf but selectively so, Aunt Agatha speaks her mind and has little time for the Warleggans, most notably the 'upstart' George Warleggan. She also dabbles in the dark art of fortune-telling, frequently muttering her gloomy predictions as she witnesses the disintegration of the Poldark family around her.

Aunt Agatha is brilliantly portrayed by Caroline Blakiston, a versatile and much revered actress of stage and screen. Her work in theatre is extensive, and previous film and television roles include Lady Patience Hardacre in *Brass*, Mon Mothma in *Star Wars: Episode VI – Return of the Jedi* and Margorie Ferrar in *The Forsyte Saga*.

AUNT AGATHA
(barely audible)
'Tis an omen, mark my words – 'tis a fiendish black omen . . .'

Fortune-telling was hugely popular in the eighteenth century, whether using Tarot cards or tea leaves.

GAMBLING

Gambling permeated much of life in the eighteenth century. From the high-stakes dice game of hazard to common drinking wagers, every class of Georgian Britain liked to have a flutter. Amongst the upper echelons of *Poldark*, card-playing is a common pursuit. When we first meet Ross, he is playing a game of French ruff with fellow soldiers. Francis also gambles away much of his family's fortune, a not uncommon occurrence in a period when the great and the good staked eye-watering amounts of money.

In London, gentleman's clubs such as White's, Boodle's and Brooks's saw huge amounts wagered. Politician Charles James Fox once played faro at Brooks's for a continuous sitting of twenty-two hours, finally leaving the table at a loss of £11,000. The Prince of Wales was famous for leading an exorbitant

Top: *'Evens and Odds' was derived from the new French game of Roulette.*
Above: *There were taxes on playing cards and dice, in an attempt to keep them out of the hands of the working classes.*

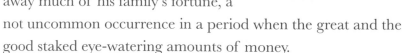

London gambling clubs kept records of wagers on the most unlikely subjects. Following the June 1785 ascent of the world's first female balloonist – actress Letitia Anne Sage, who flew with the young and wealthy Old Etonian George Biggin for company – Lord Cholmondeley of Brooks's club bet Lord Derby 500 guineas that he would manage to have sex 'in a balloon one thousand yards from the earth.' There is no record of whether he ever won the bet.

lifestyle, frittering away thousands of pounds at the races and gaming tables, 'dropping a thousand guineas at White's', says Francis in the first *Poldark* novel.

Gambling added excitement to many pastimes and almost every sport, from cock-fighting (the most popular sport of the day) and cock-throwing (in which punters threw sticks and stones at a tethered bird) to prize-fighting and coach-racing. In a bid to exploit this universal craze for gambling, the government held state lotteries, which raised huge amounts in subscriptions and helped to fund such public institutions as Westminster Bridge and the British Museum.

Popular Gambling Games
of the Eighteenth Century

CROWN AND ANCHOR A dice game popular with British sailors.
A banker rolls three dice marked with six symbols: a crown,
anchor, spade, heart, diamond and club. Players bet on which
symbols will turn up.

FARO Originated in France in the seventeenth century and
became widely popular in Europe in the eighteenth. Originally
known as pharaon, its name was shortened to pharo or faro.
Quick and easy to learn, it spread to the US in the early
nineteenth century, where it rapidly caught on with the masses
expanding westward.

FRENCH RUFF Mentioned several times during *Poldark*, and
also referred to in Shakespeare's *Antony and Cleopatra*. A
version evolved into what we now know as whist. In Winston
Graham's second novel, *Demelza*, the rules of French ruff are
given thus: 'French ruff was played with thirty-two cards,

each of the players being dealt five, and the play being as at whist except that the ace was the lowest court card. The hazard and lure of the game lay in the fact that before playing either player could discard and take up from the pack as many new cards as he chose and do this as many times as he chose, at the discretion of the nondealer.'

HAZARD An early English game (mentioned by Chaucer), played with two dice, and very popular in the seventeenth and eighteenth centuries. Hazard was played for high stakes at the tables of the London clubs. In the nineteenth century the game spread to the US where it evolved into the simpler game of craps.

LOO (LANTERLOO) The most popular card game in the eighteenth century, although it developed a bad reputation as a potentially violent 'tavern' card game in the nineteenth century.

Two views of gambling by Thomas Rowlandson. Opposite – The Gaming Table, *1801; below* – A kick-up at a Hazard Table, *1790.*

THE WARLEGGAN BANK

A key component of the Warleggan empire is its banking operation, which the family runs with ruthless efficiency. It enables the Warleggans to dominate the local economy, making or breaking local mines and businesses and killing off any competition in the process. George Warleggan slowly increases his grip on the Carnmore Copper Company by calling in the debts of some of its backers, which leads to the company's eventual closure as well as bankruptcy, debtors' prison and ruination for some of its investors.

In the second half of the eighteenth century, hundreds of country banks emerged in the provinces of Britain. They evolved out of ad-hoc banking operations set up by substantial merchants or manufacturers who perhaps held a London account and then used their accounts to undertake local business transactions on behalf of local tradesmen. Banking was therefore underpinned by a network of local contacts and business relationships, and those who operated as 'bankers' could wield great power.

The Warleggan flag, featuring a motto that is usually translated as 'Fortune favours the brave'.

A national shortage of gold and silver currency in the eighteenth century, combined with a huge expansion of trade, led to the increased use of paper 'money' in many forms.

Many provincial banks, like the Warleggans, issued their own money and bills of exchange. This expansion in the availability of capital and credit, and the development of a paper economy – in the form of bank notes, cheques and all sorts of bills of exchange passed between shopkeepers and their clients, manufacturers and their suppliers – facilitated innovation, trade and the expansion of new business. Landowners could raise money to make improvements to their estates, such as enclosing land and implementing better drainage, and local private investment in new projects could lead to the building of turnpikes and canals.

Paper bills dealt with large amounts – the lowest denomination of £10 represented half a year's pay for an average workman or two years' wages for a kitchen maid. Everyday transactions were handled in copper farthings, halfpennies and pennies, with silver shillings, half crowns and crowns (five shillings), or gold for larger amounts.

CHAPTER SEVEN

Ross is struggling to keep the Carnmore Copper Company afloat now that George is determined to crush it. After a rockfall at Wheal Leisure, Mark returns home early and discovers that Keren has been sleeping with Dwight Enys. Following an argument, Mark accidentally breaks Keren's neck, killing her. Ross helps Mark escape, only narrowly escaping arrest himself. Verity elopes with Captain Blamey, and Francis, blaming Ross for arranging the marriage, breaks with his cousin and reveals to George Warleggan the names of the Carnmore shareholders. Those who bank with the Warleggans have their debts called in and will be bankrupted. When Demelza confesses her involvement in Verity's elopement, Ross struggles to forgive her.

When Francis discovers Verity has eloped with Captain Andrew Blamey, he is furious. 'So this is how she cares for us! To sneak away under our very noses and marry that wife murdering drunkard! But how was it arranged? She must have had help.' Having expressly forbidden Verity from seeing Blamey, whom Francis believes killed his wife in a drunken rage, he jumps to the mistaken conclusion that Ross acted as go-between: 'Damn Ross! Damn this family! Damn this entire pitiful excuse for an existence!' roars Francis. Later, back at Captain Blamey's house, we see only tenderness between the couple. And when they finally marry, walking on to Andrew's ship as newlyweds, joy is written all over Verity's face; she is at last happy.

Captain Andrew Blamey is played by Welsh actor Richard Harrington.

ANDREW

'If you should ever be unhappy, my love, I swear it will not be of my doing.'

A Scandalous Marriage

The marriage of Verity and Captain Blamey was not the only one to cause scandal in the 1780s. On 15 December 1785, the Prince of Wales, the future George IV, secretly married Maria Fitzherbert. The bride was a Roman Catholic and twice married before, and the marriage, which was conducted without the King's consent contrary to the Royal Marriages Act of 1772, was illegal.

Rumours of the marriage spread, all of which were denied by politicians and the prince himself as malicious gossip. In 1795 the Prince of Wales was officially married to Princess Caroline of Brunswick, in exchange for parliament paying £600,000 of his debts (he was notoriously extravagant). Once his wife had produced an heir (Princess Charlotte, born in 1796) he and Maria were reconciled in 1800, only for her to be rejected a decade later. George's marriage to Caroline was a predictable disaster, climaxing in his attempted but failed divorce of her in 1820, and giving further ammunition to the satirists of the day.

The Fall of PHAETON *by James Gillray, 1788. The Prince of Wales is shown literally falling for Mrs Fitzherbert. The caption reads 'The imaginary Bride with Beauty glows, For Envy magnifies whate'er She shows.'*

Jacqueline at work during the first episode.

Interview with JACQUELINE FOWLER, Make-up and Hair Designer

What does your job involve?
I design the hair, make-up and prosthetics for the whole cast. Before filming, I read the scripts and novels, and I do a lot of research into the period, play around with different ideas and create mood boards for each actor. Once I've designed the look I work with a team and we source all the wigs and other items we need and attend fittings with the cast.

Wigs

In the eighteenth century, men's wigs were generally smaller than in previous eras and no longer extravagant affairs. Many were powdered a distinctive white or off-white colour, although by the 1780s wigs were increasingly the reserve of older, more conservative men. Younger men favoured their own hair, worn long, dressed and powdered (at least until the government introduced a duty on hair powder in 1795). Women wore hairpieces instead of wigs or powdered their hair for important occasions. Several professions, including the military, church and medicine, adopted wigs as part of their official costume, a practice still retained by those in the law.

What kind of wigs did you use?

We didn't want everybody in tie-backs [wigs] as it can look a bit contrived. I also didn't want any white wigs as that would have looked too Cinderella-like and we were going for more of a grey palette with the wigs. There were so many different types of male wigs in the eighteenth century – scratch wigs, pigtail wigs, military wigs and many more – and most men of status would have owned one. Different professions, such as lawyers, army officers and doctors would have worn a certain style of wig. Dr Choake's wig, for example, is a 'physical [doctor's] bob-wig'. We decided to keep the tie-backs for the older, more elite characters in the series, such as Warren Clarke, the bankers and the older gentlemen.

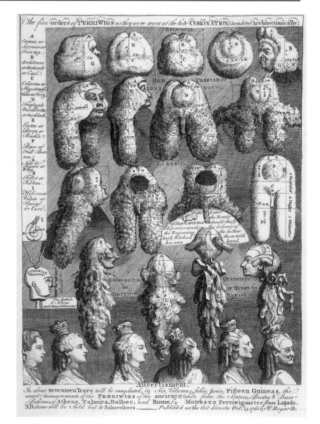

Above: *Ross before he left for America – and after his return.*
Left: The Five Orders of Periwig *by William Hogarth, 1761. This lampoons the extravagant wigs worn by some in the eighteenth century.*

How did you create Aidan Turner's look?

I came on board when they started doing the casting for the series. When I first met Aidan he had really short hair. I had a look at how he'd had it before and I thought he looked best with in-between long hair. I also had to think about his character and who Ross Poldark is. He's had money and come from quite a good background but he's lost a lot and come back from the war. When he's in the military I put him in a tie-back but I didn't give him the pipes at the side as I didn't want him to look too formal.

So Aidan had two looks – he had his earlier years with his tie-back and no scar, and then he gets his scar and comes back with his hair lopped off. We wanted to give the impression that he had just lopped off his pony tail at the back to get his messy bob look. That was the kind of man he was; unaffected and without any vanity, and he would have done something like that. Ross's longer

The Scar

In the Winston Graham novels there is no mention of which side Ross's scar is on. He returns from fighting in America 'with a scar on his cheek'. Later the scar is described as 'more than half-hidden by the long side hair, but all the same the tail of it down his cheek was a token of wildness and intractability.' Debbie Horsfield explains: 'The actual look and creation of the scar is designed by our make-up designer Jacqui Fowler who is taking as her reference the source material rather than the previous adaptation.'

hair also enabled him to fit into the world of the gentleman, as well as that of the miners who have longer hair, like him.

Aidan does have quite a bit of facial hair so I had to work on his stubble every day as I wanted it to enhance his cheek bones and bone structure. It became part of a daily ritual. I also had to trim down his chest hair. I did it all by hand from his stomach up to his neck, all with scissors. I also took out his tattoos and I put scars on his arm.

What about the scar on Aidan's face?
The face scar, which he got from a tomahawk, went from his eye down the side of his face. Sometimes you see it, sometimes you don't and I kept it very simple, and very different from the original *Poldark*, which went across the face. I also put the scar on the left side of his face. Aidan has a beautiful face and is a very good actor so I didn't want the scar to take any of that away from him.

ROSS
'Paul, Zacky, Mark, this is Dwight Enys. I have him to thank for patching me up!'

DWIGHT
'I trust my skills improved since then.'

Aidan Turner: 'There were some great moments when Eleanor and I ride together on Seamus. It can be tricky, it all depends who is on the back and it's always a rocky ride for them! Eleanor was great because she's such a good rider herself. She's confident so if the horse did anything strange she wouldn't freak out. There's something really romantic about it and it's a lovely image to watch. We'd always whisper stuff and crack each other up which was fun.'

GEORGE

'You know, one of these days you'll find yourself without means, without colleagues, without friends.

And no one to blame but yourself.'

Period paintings provided inspiration for Demelza, such as Lady Hamilton (as Nature)*, painted by George Romney (1734–1802).*
In 1782 Romney met the seventeen-year-old Emma, and went on to paint her more than sixty times. Despite being of low birth and having no education, Emma moved in the highest society — befriending royalty, marrying a British ambassador and eventually becoming the mistress of Lord Nelson.

How did you create Demelza's look?

I originally wanted Demelza to have short hair because she starts off with the urchin look, but we decided it would have looked out of place. So we went with the red hair colour, in very natural styling. And as we don't have any other red-heads in the show, her unruly red hair stands out against the green of the grass, and the blue of the sea and sky. And with Aidan being so dark, I thought it made such a wonderful contrast.

Her make-up was natural, dewy, soft-looking. We kept it very plain and simple, to bring out the best in Demelza.

Thomas Gainsborough's portraits of society ladies were invaluable reference for Elizabeth.

And Elizabeth?

Although the style for women's hair at the time was quite high, we kept Elizabeth's hair fairly low and soft. She was always immaculately turned out. We kept the bottom of her hair quite blonde and put in a few highlights and blonde undertones, to give it some interest, particularly as we had quite a few brunettes in the show and we wanted Elizabeth to stand out.

What about the other characters?

Beatie Edney, who played Prudie, has incredibly white teeth and I thought Prudie just wouldn't have those white teeth so I had some veneers made to cover them over. Demelza's father Tom Carne, played by Mark Frost, was also keen to get his pearly whites gnarled up. I gave Mark some tattoos on his hands and also on his neck.

Beauty Spots

Beauty spots or marks were a popular fashion fad in the eighteenth century. Originally used to cover up blemishes and small-pox scars, they were made out of small pieces of fine black velvet or even mouse skin (which was also used for eyebrows). Ready-made versions could also be bought in a range of shapes, from stars and hearts to crescent moons. The position of beauty marks either on the face or bosom is also said to have conveyed a secret code, such as a heart shape to the right of the cheek might convey you were married; a mark beside the mouth, will kiss but go no further, and so on.

And the party scenes?

For the make-up in *Poldark*, I generally avoided the powdered-white face look with little rosebud mouths and over the top blusher. I went for a more natural look. But at one of the Warleggan parties, we had a couple of women paled down a bit as they were guests from London, and a little more high fashion. I also put George Warleggan in a white wig.

With Margaret, the prostitute, I styled her quite over the top. We had her in a grey wig again when she became a bit more of a classy lady. She had a beauty spot, as did a few of the other prostitutes – we created them out of felt. Crystal, who played Margaret, was fantastic – she was a great canvas for me to have a bit of fun with.

Above: *Crystal Leaity as Margaret.*
Below: *The Warleggan ball.*

Loading a Smuggler, *Giles Grinagain, 1804. A sailor loads a young woman with contraband, including coffee, gin and tea (the hyson). The woman may represent the unassuming ships used to bring goods ashore, or an actual method of sneaking them past customs officers.*

SMUGGLING

When soldiers come looking for Mark after the murder of Keren, Ross's old fighting comrade Captain McNeil suggests they also look for smugglers as they search. On offering him some brandy, Ross, who has himself dabbled in 'free trade', jokes with the captain that he should be able to 'tell by the flavour whether or not the duty had been paid'.

As in *Poldark*, smuggling was very much part of life in Cornwall, the contemporary George Borlase complaining in 1753: 'The coast here swarms with smugglers from the Land's End to the Lizard, so that I wonder the soldiers (who were late quartered here) should have been ordered off without being replaced by others.' Many working Cornishmen were driven by poverty to this free trade, whilst much of the gentry and even magistrates turned a blind eye to the practice, which provided so many of life's little luxuries. As Winston Graham put it in *Ross Poldark*, Cornish society viewed the smuggler as a 'clever fellow who knew how to cheat the government of its revenues and bring them brandy at half price'.

Ships returned from France with everything from brandy, gin and salt to lace and tea. By 1770 an estimated 470,000 gallons of brandy and 350,000 pounds of tea were smuggled into Cornwall every year, whilst around 4 million gallons of gin were smuggled annually into Britain. There were violent clashes between smugglers, excisemen and troops, and the traffic in cheap spirits further exacerbated the problems of drunkenness across the country.

CHAPTER EIGHT

Ross is forced to close the Carnmore Copper Company. George shows off his new ship, the Queen Charlotte. *Trenwith is stricken with an outbreak of putrid throat, and Demelza rushes to their aid, caring for Elizabeth, Francis and Geoffrey Charles. Demelza and baby Julia become infected, Julia tragically dying in Ross's arms whilst Demelza is still delirious. Ross sees George's new ship being wrecked on rocks. He alerts the local poor and they help themselves to the cargo as it floats ashore. Ross finds George's cousin, Matthew Sanson, dead. He leads a group of survivors to safety. Demelza recovers and she and Ross grieve for Julia on the cliffs overlooking the sea. Soldiers approach and Ross is arrested for looting, inciting a riot and murder.*

SOFT *is the* WIND

As Demelza makes dough for saffron buns, she begins singing. The song continues as we see her handing out a basket of saffron buns to the miners at Wheal Leisure. Ross takes one but we sense that he hasn't yet forgiven Demelza for the rift she has caused to the family and that she is making a special effort to please him. When some ragged children run up to Ross, he gives them pieces of his bun whilst Demelza hands out the rest of the buns to the villagers.

Mem'ries like voices that call on the wind.
Medhel an gwyns, medhel an gwyns.
Whispered and tossed on the tide coming in.
Medhel, oh medhel an gwyns.

Voices like songs that are heard in the dawn,
Medhel an gwyns, medhel an gwyns.
Singing the secrets of children unborn.
Medhel, oh medhel an gwyns.

Songs like the dream that the bal maidens spin,
Medhel an gwyns, medhel an gwyns.
Weaving the song of the cry of the tin.
Medhel, oh medhel an gwyns.

Dreams, like the castles that sleep in the sand,
Medhel an gwyns, medhel an gwyns.
Slip through the fingers or held in the hand.
Medhel, oh medhel an gwyns.

Dreams like the memories once borne on the wind.
Medhel an gwyns, medhel an gwyns.
Lovers and children and copper and tin,
Medhel, oh medhel an gwyns.
Medhel, oh medhel an gwyns.

Secrets like stories that no one has told.
Medhel an gwyns, medhel an gwyns.
Stronger than silver and brighter than gold.
Medhel, oh medhel an gwyns.

M. J. O'Connor

The music and lyrics for 'Medhel an gwyns' were written by the Cornish folk musician and musicologist Mike O'Connor. The Kernewek (Cornish language) refrain *medhel an gwyns* literally means 'soft [is] the wind'. (The 'dh' sound is a 'soft th', as in them, not as in thistle.)

The words of the song take you through the whole landscape of *Poldark* as if you are being conveyed on a gentle wind. In mid-Cornwall, where *Poldark* is set, Cornish was rarely spoken but as Mike O'Connor explains, 'Demelza is from Illogan, which is that bit further west, so in my mind's eye I thought she might have remembered the odd bit of Cornish that perhaps her mother had spoken.'

Along with Merv Davey (see page 136), Mike also advised on the types of songs sung by groups of miners in Poldark *and even by the drunken Jud, all of which were authentic Cornish folk songs.*

Asked to write tunes that were both authentic-sounding and had the feel of traditional folk songs, Mike also composed the music for 'I Pluck a Fair Rose' as sung by Demelza during Christmas celebrations at Trenwith, as well as the various songs that Demelza sings as she goes about her domestic chores.

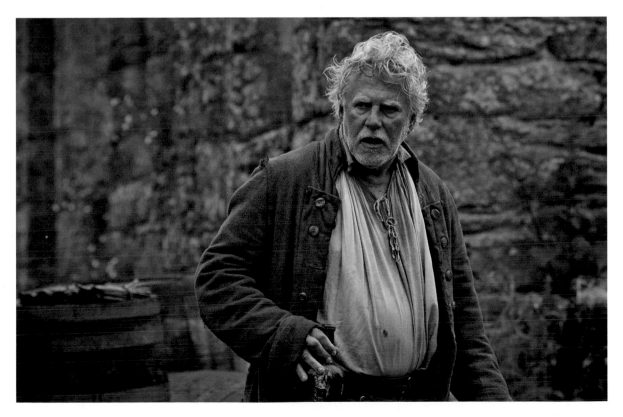

WRECKING

In a gathering storm, the Warleggan ship, the *Queen Charlotte*, is wrecked on the rocks off Hendrawna Beach. This is land belonging to Ross Poldark and he immediately rides off to tell the villagers, who come down to the beach and help drag in the ship's cargo.

Over the centuries, the treacherous coast of Cornwall has led to countless shipwrecks, deemed by those that found them as theirs for the taking. Indeed it was the common-held belief that the contents of any wreck washing up on shore were the landowner's by legal right.

The annals of Cornwall tell of numerous similar incidents, of 'half-starved tynners' stripping off a wreck with picks and axes – and with many barely scratching a living it's no wonder they viewed a shipwreck as a gift of God. Between 1764 and 1778 at least three ships ran aground on Perranporth Beach, where

The Shipwreck, Claude-Joseph Vernet, 1772. *Cornwall has a rocky coast, prevailing onshore winds and busy shipping routes to the north and south – so the prevalence of wrecks before the development of efficient lighthouses is unsurprising.*

William McGregor, Block Two Poldark *Director: 'I loved filming in the Cornish landscape; it's such a beautiful and dramatic world for a story to be set in. I particularly enjoyed shooting the shipwreck sequence at Jangye Ryn. A series of epic night shoots on a spectacular beach with hundreds of crew and extras illuminated by the glowing blaze of our wreck.'*

Catrin Meredydd: 'The ship itself was done with visual effects – VFX. We sourced lots of paintings that were used to help create the ship. Then we had to make a lot of debris to float up on the beach. We did lose a few barrels, I think. That was a hard couple of nights, that shoot. But it looks great on screen.'

Winston Graham himself later lived. In 1764 the entire cargo of a French ship wrecked on the beach went in half a day, and two or three years later, in nearby Porthleven, miners cleared a Dutch ship of claret in a day. In 1778, two ships ran aground on Perranporth Beach, and reports of the subsequent wrecking and rioting of miners on the beach provided Winston Graham with the basis for the shipwrecks in the novel *Demelza*.

Putrid Throat

'Putrid throat' breaks out amongst the villagers and at Trenwith. In the eighteenth century putrid throat, or morbid throat, was probably a catch-all term for a variety of illnesses: in *Poldark* those infected suffer from severe sore throats and difficulty in swallowing, followed by high fever and delirium. This could indicate diphtheria, a highly contagious bacterial infection that mainly affects the nose and throat. Today there are vaccines and treatment for diphtheria but in the eighteenth century doctors could do little to fight it (although Dr Choake no doubt resorted to a bit of a leeching). It was greatly feared as one of the most common causes of death, killing almost all of the children it affected. The death of baby Julia was a tragic but sadly all-too-common event in eighteenth-century Britain.

Domestic Medicine, 1772
[Description] of the Putrid, Ulcerous Sore Throat

This has been very fatal in the more southern counties. Children are more subject to it than adults, females than males, and the delicate more than those who are hardy and robust. It prevails most in autumn, or after a long course of damp or sultry weather.

CAUSES
This is evidently a contagious distemper and is generally communicated by infection. Whole families, and even entire villages often receive the infection from one person. This ought to put people upon their guard against going near such patients as labour under the disorder . . .

REGIMEN
- *The patient must be kept quiet and for the most part in bed, as he will be apt to faint when taken out of it.*
- *His food must be nourishing and restorative, strong broths with red wine, jellies &c. His drink ought to be generous and of an antiseptic quality; as red wine negas, white wine whey and the such like.*

If great weakness and dejection of spirits or night sweats with other symptoms of a consumption should remain after this disease we would advise the patient to continue the use of the Peruvian bark, with the elixir of vitriol and to take frequently a glass of generous wine. These, together with a milk-diet, and riding on horseback are the most likely means for recovering his strength.

ANNE DUDLEY – *POLDARK* MUSIC COMPOSER

The beautiful and haunting music of *Poldark* was created by the critically acclaimed musician Anne Dudley. A founding member of The Art of Noise, Anne has composed music for countless film and television programmes, contributed string arrangements to many albums, composed an opera with Terry Jones and won an Oscar, a Grammy, a Brit and several Ivor Novello nominations. With this impressive CV, she was very keen to work on *Poldark*, as she explains:

'I found out there was going to be a new adaptation of *Poldark* and I had a vague memory of the '70s series and that it had a romantic hero and was set in Cornwall. So I was intrigued and I asked my agent if they could get hold of some scripts. I read Debbie's first three scripts and I couldn't put it down. I was so taken by the atmosphere, and the ways she brought the characters vividly to life. In my head it was already writing itself. I thought, I've got to do this!'

As soon as Anne was on board, she went down to the
Trenwith set to meet Debbie and producer Karen Thrussell and
to get a feel for the series. Once filming was done, she set about
creating the music for the series' opening credits and general
soundtrack, all of which provided a critical element in setting the
mood, pace and tone of *Poldark*.

'The music needed to underscore the sweeping Cornish
landscapes and passionate love story. Featuring the solo violin,
it is based loosely on the modality found in Cornish folk music.
There's this fantastic collection of music, "Songs of the West",
which features hundreds of songs from Devon and Cornwall
as collected and notated by a nineteenth-century clergyman. I
took on board certain characteristics of the music, to include its
modal scale, although the music also needs to appeal to modern
sensibilities.

'There's lots of other things going on in the *Poldark* music
as well – it was orchestrated for violin, harp, piano, a string
orchestra and occasional electronic elements. In the title

sequence, there are lots of shots of the sea so we have a piano riff which is supposed to represent the crashing of waves.

'I wanted also to find a sound that would be characteristic of Ross himself so I used a solo violin for that. It's played by a friend, Chris Garrick. He plays jazz and folk fiddle, so he gives the music an earthy feel. It also has a very characteristic, expressive feel about it. The producers were a bit unsure about the solo violin at first but I think they were taken by it once they heard Chris play. He played it on a five-string violin and in a lower register in some scenes, to include when Ross first comes home and when baby Julia dies and Demelza lets the keepsake ribbon fly off.

'What's also great about *Poldark* is that there are long sequences where nobody says anything. So there's lots of room for the music to say something. Most television series have wall-to-wall speaking but with *Poldark*, they still manage to have pace to it but it has these great periods of landscape shots, and cutting between scenes. And that's why it's so interesting to do the music for it. It makes it more filmic and helps to define the characters in the story.'

Interview with MARIANNE AGERTOFT, Costume Designer

How did you prepare for working on Poldark*?*

The first step was to get familiar with the scripts and figure out what the characters required in terms of costume. You then need to learn about the era, which often involves looking at paintings from the period as well as trying to find out how people actually lived at the time. I was very lucky because a costume lecturer I know came and helped us out. I also looked at original garments and pattern books from the time.

It's important to surround yourself with knowledgeable people – we had a fantastic team of costume makers on board who understand the era and how clothes should be cut. There are relatively few costume dramas set in the 1780s, and with less stock available a large number of costume makes were required. The details of the garments that were made for the cast were exquisite, from the fantastic cuts to the delicate, detailed hand embroidery.

Right: Portrait of an Unknown Man, *c. 1777. This young man inspired the look of Ross Poldark. The Italian painting was found on a British ship captured by the French in 1779 and claimed as a prize of war. The ship's contents were sold to the Spanish King Carlos III.*

What happens next?

Once we've met the actors we then think further about the look of each character and choose the colour, fabric and texture for their costumes. Fabrics were chosen with great care and dyed to fit the palette of the Cornish landscape. The colours of the costumes have to suit individual actors, but they also need to work within the sets and the many natural locations of *Poldark*.

We then do fittings with principal cast and think more about the fall and cut of their clothes and how they look on individual cast members. The aim with all of this is to provide the actors with a wardrobe that they feel at ease in and that they feel belongs to the character they are playing.

The Peasant's Family *by John Opie provided inspiration for Demelza's costumes. Opie was the son of a Truro carpenter but a local doctor recognized his natural talent as an artist and encouraged him to switch trades. After painting many local Cornish people he moved to London aged twenty and completed hundreds of portraits, including Mary Shelley and Samuel Johnson.*

This self-portrait from 1791 by Rose-Adélaïde Ducreux (1761–1802) was used as inspiration for Elizabeth's ballgown.

The *Poldark* scripts have a very timeless feel and rather than being overly pedantic about period accuracy, the priority is to make the costumes look and feel relevant, both to the cast wearing them and to the audience watching.

How important was the location of Cornwall?
Cornwall's main port town of Truro would have been influenced by other cultures, including London, but not necessarily in an overtly fashionable way. A mix of sailors, traders, farmers, fishermen, soldiers and local gentry all gathered in one place, giving great variety.

When creating a fictional world it is important to balance the levels of society so they appear to inhabit the same world and the audience can relate to it. I need to have a clear vision of the look of the supporting artists, in order to harmonize that with the designs for the principal cast.

What was it like filming in Cornwall?
I was aware that we would be filming outside a lot in Cornwall and that interior shots would be quite dark. So we had to put a lot of work into this. If you're filming outside in nature, when it's really sunny, even the most beautiful silk can look too shiny. And you don't want the costumes to look too theatrical. One of Elizabeth's dresses – the pink one with circles – just didn't work outside, so you have to be really careful about this.

How did you create Ross Poldark's look?

Ross is a man who doesn't worry about how he looks, so I wanted his clothes to be simple and unfussy. Aidan had so much on his plate. He needed to feel good about what he was wearing. We had to ensure he could move in his costume, and we spent a lot of time trying to get the cut right in his trousers so he can kick over a horse.

Originally, I had browner/greener colours in mind for him but I realized that I needed to keep his colours fairly cool and neutral, and I wanted to use colours that worked well with his skin tone.

Whilst it looks like Ross rarely changes his clothes, I did make a few changes. He has a blue frock coat (worn I think when he goes to town) which doesn't have a stand-up collar. But as the series progresses and he's at the Warleggan ball and then at the funeral, his frock coat has got a higher collar, which is a really elegant look and frames the face beautifully. I'm not always there during filming so it's important the actors are really familiar with their own wardrobe.

And Demelza?

I knew Eleanor from working on *Death Comes to Pemberley* so we already had a good working relationship. The journey she takes in *Poldark* had to be decided at a very early stage, so Eleanor could envisage that journey from the outset. Demelza first appears dressed as a boy – originally she had a little jacket on but Ed the director suggested we take it off.

After her fight, Demelza loses the buttons on her shirt and as she doesn't change out of this for a while, it leaves her a bit exposed. So she holds

herself a little differently when wearing this shirt in order to cover herself.

When she starts to wear dresses and skirts, like the red skirt Prudie gives her and the yellow stripy dress, she continues to wear breeches underneath. We thought she wouldn't be the kind of girl to wear petticoats and she needed to be comfortable riding a horse. There's a scene when she's walking on a beach with Garrick the dog and she has her breeches on with her dress tied up a bit. Once she's out of the breeches, you'll notice she rides side-saddle (as it's really uncomfortable riding astride without any underwear on!).

Initially we used strips of gauze to flatten her bosom, but gradually we wanted to show off her gorgeous figure. When she's a mother, she wore jumps, which gave her bosom a more natural shape.

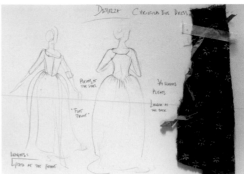

As Demelza becomes aware of her sexuality, she begins to enjoy dressing as a woman and takes pride in herself, but in a modest and simple way. The choice of fabrics and colours reflects her love of nature.

The Christmas dress is Demelza's own choice of dress. It has simple but beautifully detailed fabric with little flowers and delicate embroidery. When she sings at the Christmas party, we can see the wonderful detail of the dress.

The Warleggan ball gown is a dress Ross chose and had made for her, and I don't think Demelza would have chosen such a rich fabric. It's quite a simple dress so it's the fabric that makes her stand out at the Warleggan ball.

Demelza's ball gown (left) and Christmas party dress (right).

Above right: The Linley Sisters (Mrs. Sheridan and Mrs. Tickell) *by Thomas Gainsborough 1771/72.*

And Elizabeth?

For Elizabeth, and much of *Poldark*, we were really inspired by the classic portraits of the era, such as by Thomas Gainsborough, Sir Joshua Reynolds and George Romney. The details on the dusty pink/mauve gown came from studying those paintings as well as looking at original garments and their patterns. As Lady Poldark of Trenwith her outfits are elegant but simple, visually still fitting into Ross's more down-to-earth world.

We tried a few variations with Elizabeth and once we found a shape that suited Heida, all her dresses were based on that. I also worked really hard on getting the colours just right – we actually had to dye a dress we'd already made, which is a bit nerve-wracking and something we wouldn't normally do.

What about the villagers and mining families?

This is a world that Ross moves in and you need to believe that the villagers and miners are his friends. Our aim always was to create a world in which the audience could relate to all the social levels and just enjoy the story as it unfolds.

It was a key requirement of the brief to create a unique look for the miners with interesting rich textures. The miners' work wear had authentic details like the fire-proof felt hats holding the wax candles. These were custom-made for the production along with other accessories.

A lot of work went into ageing the miners' and villagers' costumes to create greater depth and texture.

Left: A Gentleman and a Miner with a Specimen of Copper Ore *by John Opie (1761–1807). The earthy atmosphere of Cornish painter John Opie's painting was the basis of the more realistic feel of the costumes.*

Below left: *Zacky and Mrs Martin, played by Tristan Sturrock and Emma Spurgin Hussey.*

Below centre: *Paul Daniel, played by Ed Browning.*

Below right: *George Warleggan and his cousin Matthew Sanson, played by Jason Thorpe.*

And the Warleggans?

The Warleggan circle depict the wealthy gentry of Cornwall. They reflect the world of fashion, initially in quite a restrained manner, but as their wealth grows, they become more flamboyant and ostentatious. There is a different edge to George Warleggan but I didn't want to go too far with his look, I didn't want him to look too much of a dandy. Ross, Francis and George need to have a fairly similar look, they grew up together after all, and male dress in this era was increasingly minimal so I didn't go to town with them.

I did have a bit more fun with George's cousin, however, Matthew Sanson. I threw in a bit of frou-frou as he has come from London and is from a more fashionable set.

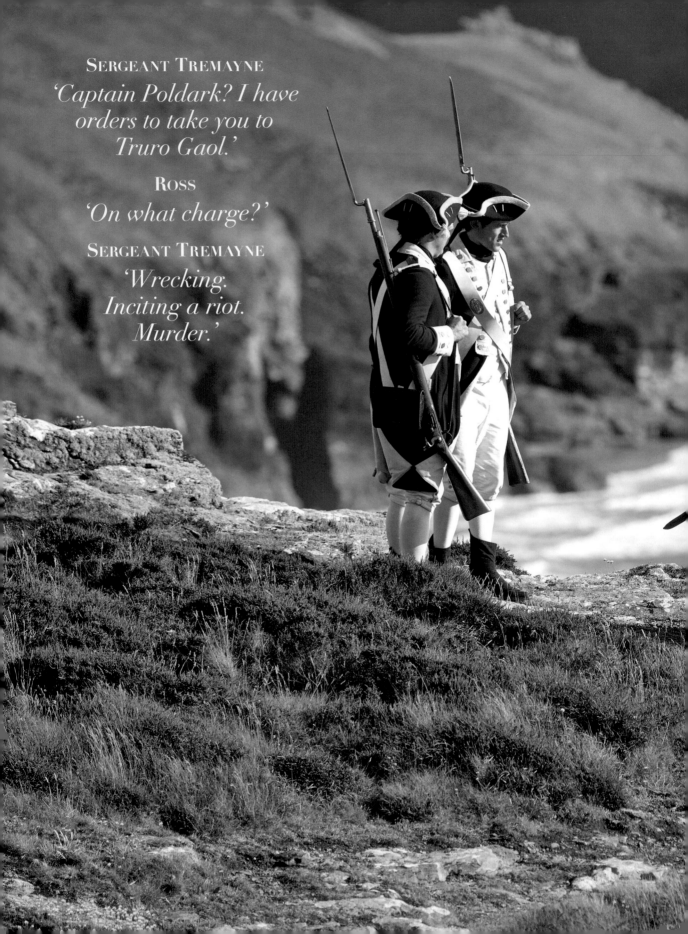

SERGEANT TREMAYNE

'Captain Poldark? I have orders to take you to Truro Gaol.'

ROSS

'On what charge?'

SERGEANT TREMAYNE

'Wrecking. Inciting a riot. Murder.'

*'Tis a mistake! –
you cannot believe it –
Ross, tell him!'*

Afterword

September 2015: the cast assemble for a read-through of the second series of *Poldark*. Screenwriter Debbie Horsfield watches nervously as her words are unveiled for the first time. Executive producer Karen Thrussell is similarly excited about the next series, which promises to be bigger and better than the first. Amongst the cast new and familiar faces greet each other, anticipating the start of filming in Cornwall the following week. At the centre of it all, between Eleanor and Heida, sits Aidan – primed and ready once again to take on the role of Captain Ross Poldark.

KEY CAST

Ross Poldark	AIDAN TURNER
Demelza Carne	ELEANOR TOMLINSON
Jud Paynter	PHIL DAVIS
Prudie Paynter	BEATIE EDNEY
George Warleggan	JACK FARTHING
Elizabeth Chynoweth	HEIDA REED
Francis Poldark	KYLE SOLLER
Charles Poldark	WARREN CLARKE
Verity Poldark	RUBY BENTALL
Captain Andrew Blamey	RICHARD HARRINGTON
Dwight Enys	LUKE NORRIS
Aunt Agatha	CAROLINE BLAKISTON
Cary Warleggan	PIP TORRENS
Dr Choake	ROBERT DAWS
Reverend Halse	ROBIN ELLIS
Jim Carter	ALEXANDER ARNOLD
Jinny Carter	GRACEE O'BRIEN
Keren Smith	SABRINA BARTLETT
Mark Daniel	MATTHEW WILSON
Captain Henshawe	JOHN HOLLINGWORTH
Richard Tonkin	RORY WILTON
Blight	BILLY GERAGHTY
Matthew Sanson	JASON THORPE
Margaret	CRYSTAL LEAITY
Ruth Teague	HARRIET BALLARD
Mrs Chynoweth	SALLY DEXTER
Harris Pascoe	RICHARD HOPE
Tom Carne	MARK FROST
Zacky Martin	TRISTAN STURROCK
Mrs Zacky Martin	EMMA SPURGIN HUSSEY
Paul Daniel	ED BROWNING
Horace Treneglos	MICHAEL CULKIN
John Treneglos	DANIEL COOK
Sir Hugh Bodrugan	PATRICK RYECART
Harry Blewitt	HYWEL SIMONS
Captain McNeil	HENRY GARRETT

KEY CREW

Screenwriter and Executive Producer
DEBBIE HORSFIELD

Directors
ED BAZALGETTE and
WILLIAM McGREGOR

Producer
ELIZA MELLOR

Consultant
ANDREW GRAHAM

Casting Director
SUSIE PARRISS

Make-up & Hair Designer
JACQUELINE FOWLER

Costume Designer
MARIANNE AGERTOFT

Music by
ANNE DUDLEY

Editors
ADAM RECHT A.C.E.
ADAM GREEN
ROBIN HILL

Directors of Photography
CINDERS FORSHAW B.S.C.
ADAM ETHERINGTON

Production Designer
CATRIN MEREDYDD

Executive Producers
DEBBIE HORSFIELD
KAREN THRUSSELL
DAMIEN TIMMER

ACKNOWLEDGEMENTS

A huge thanks to Dan Newman who designed this book but also provided so much more, from extra bits of material (to include the interview with Catrin Meredydd) to picture sourcing as well as invaluable support, feedback and friendship throughout the creation of this book and many projects over the years. Thanks also to Georgina Morley for her trust, support and humour, Nicholas Blake for his editorial expertise, Zennor Compton for being an all-round star, as well as all the good eggs at Macmillan including Charlotte Wright, Ena Matagic and Jeremy Trevathan.

Huge thanks also to Andrew and Peggotty Graham for their good will, support and expertise on all things *Poldark*, as well as Dr Hannah Greig who provided invaluable information about the eighteenth-century world.

Many thanks to Shirley Patton at ITV for her support and to the hugely talented team at Mammoth Screen who have allowed me to write about their world and have been encouraging and helpful throughout: in particular Karen Thrussell as well as James Penny, Melanie Morris, Charlotte Frings, Michael Ray and Margaret Mitchell. Many thanks also to Jacqueline Fowler, Marianne Agertoft, Catrin Meredydd, Debbie Horsfield, Anne Dudley, Mike O'Connor, Merv Davey, Joanna Booth, Robert Daws and Luke Norris, all of whom generously gave their time to talk or write about their involvement in the making of the television series.

And a heartfelt thank you to Winston Graham, who gave us Ross, Demelza and the incredible world of *Poldark*.

PICTURE CREDITS

All pictures courtesy of Mammoth Screen Limited except the following:
Bridgeman Images: pp43, 168 (left), 215, 216
Anne Dudley: p201
J. Paul Getty Museum's Open Content Program: p107
Andrew Graham: p32
The Lewis Walpole Library, Yale University: pp168 (right), 173, 190, 191
Library of Congress: pp43, 108, 178, 205
Mary Evans Picture Library 2015: pp92, 130, 134, 135
Museo de la Real Academia de Bellas Artes de San Fernando, Madrid: p205
National Gallery of Art, Washington: pp189 (all), 198
National Trust, Waddesdon Manor: p208 bottom right
Perfect Bound Ltd: p220 (both)
Shutterstock.com/Everett Historical: p21
Shutterstock.com/Helen Hotson: pp36, 52, 95
Shutterstock.com/ian woolcock: pp115, 132
Shutterstock.com/Philip Bird LRPS CPAGB: p151
Tate, London 2015: pp63, 206
Victorian Picture Library: p69
Wikimedia Commons: pp106, 118, 119, 180
Wikimedia Commons/Metropolitan Museum of Art, New York: p207
Wikimedia Commons/The Frick Collection: p186
Yale Center for British Art: pp41, 91, 93, 107, 131, 171, 172

First published 2015 by Macmillan
an imprint of Pan Macmillan
20 New Wharf Road, London N1 9RR
Associated companies throughout the world
www.panmacmillan.com

ISBN 978-1-250-10271-3 (hardcover)
ISBN 978-1-250-10272-0 (e-book)

Copyright text © Pan Macmillan 2015

Copyright foreword, programme and photographs © Mammoth Screen Ltd 2015

Ross Poldark novel quotations © Winston Graham 1945

BBC and the BBC logo are trade marks of the British Broadcasting Corporation and are used under licence. Logo © BBC 1996

The World of Poldark. All rights reserved. For information, address St. Martin's Press, 175 Fifth Avenue, New York, N.Y. 10010.

A Mammoth Screen production for BBC and MASTERPIECE™

Poldark is available on Blu-ray and DVD. To purchase, visit shopPBS.org.

MASTERPIECE™ is a trademark of the WGBH Educational Foundation. Used with permission.

The PBS Logo is a registered trademark of the Public Broadcasting Service and used with permission.

www.stmartins.com

The Library of Congress Cataloging-in-Publication Data is available upon request

Our books may be purchased in bulk for promotional, educational, or business use. Please contact your local bookseller or the Macmillan Corporate and Premium Sales Department at (800) 221-7945, extension 5442, or by e-mail at MacmillanSpecialMarkets@macmillan.com.

First U.S. Edition: May 2016

10 9 8 7 6 5 4 3 2 1

Project managed by Emma Marriott
Designed by Perfect Bound Ltd

Printed and bound in Italy